Digital Composition

Book Clubs

ESSAY

POETRY

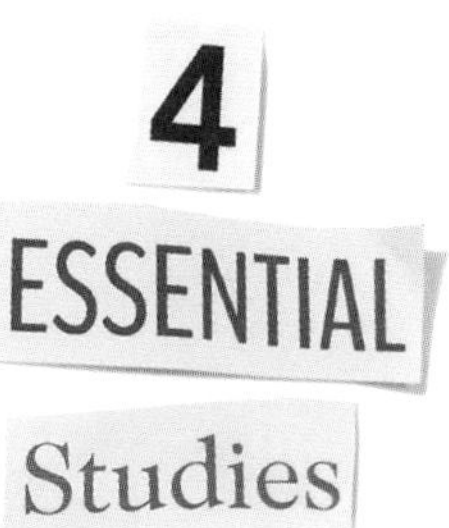
4
ESSENTIAL
Studies

Penny Kittle · Kelly Gallagher

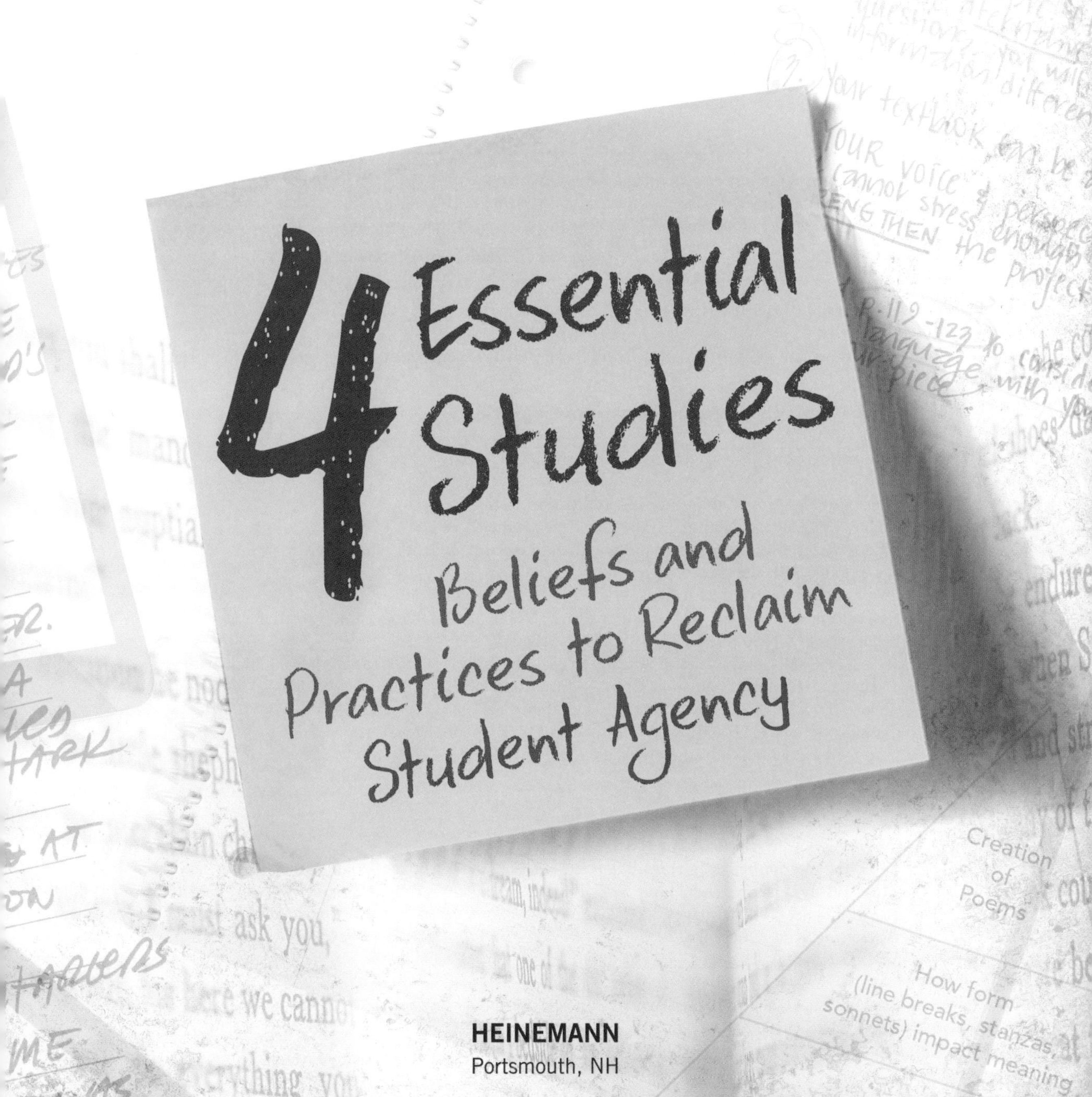

4 Essential Studies

Beliefs and Practices to Reclaim Student Agency

HEINEMANN
Portsmouth, NH

Heinemann
145 Maplewoood Avenue, Suite 300
Portsmouth, NH 03801
www.heinemann.com

Offices and agents throughout the world

The authors and publisher wish to thank those who have generously given permission to reprint borrowed material:

Figure 1–3, "America, Reloading" by Andrea Gibson, Courtesy of Button Publishing Inc., Copyright 2018.

Acknowledgments for borrowed material continue on p. xxiii.

Library of Congress Cataloging-in-Publication Data
Names: Kittle, Penny, author. | Gallagher, Kelly, author.
Title: 4 essential studies : beliefs and practices to reclaim student agency / Penny Kittle and Kelly Gallagher.
Other titles: Four essential studies.
Description: Portsmouth, NH : Heinemann, 2021. | Includes bibliographical references.
Identifiers: LCCN 2021020558 | ISBN 9780325120065
Subjects: LCSH: Composition (Language arts)—Study and teaching (Secondary). | English language—Composition and exercises—Study and teaching (Secondary). | Essay. | Book clubs (Discussion groups). | Poetry. | Digital media.
Classification: LCC LB1631 .K539 2021 | DDC 372.62/3—dc23
LC record available at https://lccn.loc.gov/2021020558

Editor: Thomas Newkirk
Production: Vicki Kasabian
Cover and text designs: Suzanne Heiser
Cover and interior images: girl reading poetry book © Johner Images/Alamy Stock Photo; hands writing essay © Jacob Lund/Alamy Stock Photo; reading circle © benis arapovic/Alamy Stock Photo; boy with tablet © Tetra Images, LLC/Alamy Stock Photo; green post-it © Chaisi/Adobe Stock
Typesetting: Kim Arney
Manufacturing: Val Cooper

Printed in the United States of America on acid-free paper
1 2 3 4 5 CGB 26 25 24 23 22 21
September 2021 Printing

FOUR ESSENTIAL STUDIES

OUR FOUNDATION

We thank the following people, who have influenced our thinking over the course of our careers and without whom this book would not have been possible.

Aeriale Johnson · Alfie Kohn · Alfred Tatum · Anne Atwell Merkel · Arthur Applebee · Barry Lane · Bob Probst · Carl Anderson · Carol Booth Olson · Carol Jago · Chad Everett · Chris Crutcher · Clint Smith · Colleen Cruz · Constance Weaver · Cornelius Minor · Cris Tovani · Dan Feigelson · Dana Johansen · David Bayles · David Conley · Donald Graves · Donald Murray · Donalyn Miller · Donna Santman · E. D. Hirsch · Elaine Millen · Elizabeth Rossini · Ellin Keene · Erik Palmer · Ernest Morrell · Gay Ivey · Georgia Heard · Gholdy Muhammad · Grant Wiggins · Greg Lukianoff · Ibram X. Kendi · James Britton · James Moffett · Janet Allen · Jeff Anderson · Jeff McQuillan · Jeff Wilhelm · Jim Burke · Jim Cummins · Jim Trelease · John Dewey · John Powers · John Warner · Jonathan Haidt · Jonathan Kozol · Jonathan Lovell · Judith Langer · Julia Torres · Julie Wright · Katherine Bomer · Kathy Collins · Katie Wood Ray · Kim Parker · Kylene Beers · Kwame Alexander · Laura Robb · Lily King · Linda Rief · Liz Prather · Lois Bridges · Louise Rosenblatt · Lucy Calkins · Lydia Davis · Lynda Barry · Maja Wilson · Mary K. Healy · Matt Glover · Matthew Kay · Mike Schmoker · Nancie Atwell · Parker Palmer · Patti Stock · Paulo Freire · Pedro Noguera · Pernille Ripp · Peter Elbow · Peter Johnston · Ralph Fletcher · Randy Bomer · Regie Routman · Richard Allington · Rick Wormeli · Robert Marzano · Robin Turner · Samantha Bennett · Sara Ahmed · Sarah Zerwin · Shelley Harwayne · Sheridan Blau · Smokey Daniels · Sonja Cherry-Paul · Stephanie Harvey · Stephen Krashen · Sylvan Barnet · Ted Orland · Ted Sizer · Teri Lesesne · Thomas C. Foster · Tom Newkirk · Tom Romano · Tomasen Carey · Tricia Ebarvia · Yong Zhao · our students

The means are not important; to alienate human beings from their own decision-making is to change them into objects.

—Paulo Friere, *Pedagogy of the Oppressed*

Education should not be intended to make people comfortable; it is meant to make them think.

—Hanna Holborn Gray, *Searching for Utopia*

The true path to progress is not paved with certainty but doubt, with being "open to revision."

—Lulu Miller, *Why Fish Don't Exist*

Online Resources xiii
Acknowledgments xv

Introduction *Who Is Making the Decisions?* xix

1 ◈ Teaching the ESSAY as an Art Form 1

Our Beliefs About Teaching Essay Writing 3
Practices Most Important in Teaching the Essay 12
Assessment and Grading 37
Closing Thoughts 43

2 ◈ Book Clubs: The Best Teacher of Reading Is the Reading 44

Our Beliefs About Book Clubs 45
Practices Most Important in Teaching Book Clubs 52
Assessment and Grading 74
Closing Thoughts 76

3 ◈ Poetry: The Potential for Unexpected Things 80

Our Beliefs About Teaching Poetry 81
Practices Most Important in Teaching Poetry 87
Assessment and Grading 106
Closing Thoughts 113

4 ◈ Digital Composition: Crossing Genre Boundaries 116

Our Beliefs About Teaching Digital Composition 117
Practices Most Important in Teaching Digital Composition 126
Assessment and Grading 140
Closing Thoughts 144

Last Words 147
Works Cited 153

CHAPTER 2

Two-Page Spread with Lists: OR 2–1 (Figure 2–9a)

Two-Page Spread with Sticky Notes Transferred from the Book: OR 2–2 (Figure 2–9b)

Two-Page Spread Organized with Different-Colored Sticky Notes: OR 2–3 (Figure 2–9c)

Two-Page Spread with Highlighted Points: OR 2–4 (Figure 2–9d)

Two-Page Spread with Guiding Questions at Top: OR 2–5 (Figure 2–9e)

Two-Page Spread on Human Tissue: OR 2–6 (Figure 2–9f)

CHAPTER 3

What Kelly Learned About Teaching While Writing a Poem: OR 3–1 (Figure 3–5)

How Students Were Inspired by a Poet's Craft Moves: OR 3–2 (Figure 3–6)

Poetry Survey: OR 3–3 (Figure 3–8)

Descriptors of Excellence for Digital Movies: OR 3–4 (Figure 3–9)

Descriptors of Excellence for Voice Recordings: OR 3–5 (Figure 3–10)

Online Resources for *4 Essential Studies* can be found under Companion Resources at http://hein.pub/4studies

Acknowledgments

From Penny

Whenever I finish writing an article or a book, I wish some people I've lost were here to celebrate with me: Don Graves, Don Murray, and my dad. But I'm grateful, always, for other companions who regularly share the ongoing struggle to write with me: Linda Rief, Tom Romano, and Georgia Heard. Writing feels impossible most of the time, but they remind me of its rewards.

Tom Newkirk has shepherded my career through imagining first books and keynotes to wrestling over book titles and the tone of a paragraph. Tom has guided my thinking for years, from teaching UNH summer courses I've attended to coediting a collection of Don Graves' work with me. Meetings at his house always include book recommendations, serious scholarship, baseball talk, and laughter. Tom loves to learn. I have been blessed to have been in his company and certainly to have my writing edited by him.

I want to acknowledge what a gift it is to be in the company of teachers when I sit at my desk before light, writing to you. There is an intimate space between my wobbly thoughts and a conversation I imagine we are having. Your warm welcome at conferences and your many, many kindnesses sustain my commitment to words on the page.

My crew of friends at the Book Love Foundation are beautiful people, selfless and determined. Thank you to Elaine Millen, Clare Landrigan, Yukari Ohno, Julia Torres, Kylene Beers, Chelsea Papineau, and Paul Chant. To our grant recipients: your commitment to equity and children inspires me.

My students at Kennett High School in North Conway, New Hampshire, and now at Plymouth State University have kept me grounded in the difference between theory and practice. They humble and encourage me; they teach me what matters. Huge gratitude to friends and colleagues in both places: Melissa Cyr, Taylor Kanzler, Ed Fayle, Jack Loynd, Ryan Mahan, John Weitz, and Elliott Gruner. You are always up for intellectual conversations about learning (and wine and paddleboarding and dogs and music).

My family is my constant joy. Cam is always curious about my work. He's not just an exceptional listener but also a generous father and son. Hannah shares her delights and her burdens as an early career teacher, and we learn, cook, and wonder together. Ellen is committed to the care of this world and all its people, working to finish her degree in social work while she also mothers my brilliant, giggling grandchildren: Maisie and Lila. And my husband, Pat, waits (almost patiently) for me to let go of a project, so we can be back in the woods with headlamps and snowshoes or on the water, silently paddling side by side. The love and support of my family are braided into every word I write.

And Kelly Gallagher.

Imagine you've come to the end of a long run and face one last hill. (I can picture one just outside of Clatskanie, Oregon, on a misty Saturday morning.) It's so steep and you're so tired. You need a companion who refuses to let you give up and who makes lists of deadlines (even if you refuse to read them) to keep you on pace. You need someone who knows you well enough to recognize your most skillful evasive maneuvers and to steer you back on task. You need someone who listens with kindness when you have to drop this project for days at a time. I wish you all a writing companion and friend like Kelly. He is the reason we turned this in *before* our deadline.

From Kelly

At the 2010 NCTE conference in Orlando, Heinemann arranged a lunch so that I could meet one of my educational heroes, Tom Newkirk. As I walked into the meeting, I had only one thought: *Do not say anything stupid.* We started by discussing baseball, and a friendship began (despite Tom's allegiance to the Red Sox). Flash forward to 2021, and Tom has edited this book. If you had told me years ago that Tom Newkirk would someday be our editor, I would have immediately driven you to the nearest urgent care facility. Truly, this has been a wonderful and surreal experience. Tom, thank you for your wisdom and guidance, both in making this a much better book and in all you have done to be a voice of reason in our profession.

When this manuscript was turned in, my wife, Kristin, said to me, "Welcome back!" I asked her what she meant, and she replied, "Even when you were not writing, you were writing." I hereby plead guilty, and would like to acknowledge how deeply appreciative I am of the patience, love, and support she gave during the two years of writing this book. I also send my love to my beautiful daughters, Caitlin and Devin. I love you like pigs love pies.

Thank you to my colleagues at Magnolia High School, most notably my lunch table crew: Michelle Waxman, Robin Turner, Katrina Mundy, Lindsay Paananen, Kalli Pappas, and Taylor Thorne. What an honor to work with such caring, committed educators and accomplished punsters. Shout-outs as well to my district-level colleagues who supported me as I began this project, specifically Michael Matsuda, Jaron Fried, Manuel Colon, Jackie Counts, and Mike Switzer. Tracy, I'm glad you like my desk. You're welcome, Mitch.

Deep thanks and appreciation to my former students at Magnolia High School. You inspired me daily with your humanity and perseverance. I count myself fortunate to have been a small part of your journey.

Last, I'd like to acknowledge that this book was written in a dark time. Fortunately, I was tethered to a beacon of light. Her name is Penny Kittle, and it is hard to put into words how much our daily conversations meant to me. There were mornings when I thought I didn't have the bandwidth to talk, let alone write, but this always changed every time we started talking. I am fortunate to have a friend and writing partner who is such a compassionate human being. Writing a book with Penny Kittle means being in a two-year conversation with one of the most brilliant, forward-thinking educators in the land. It doesn't get better than that.

From both of us

We were delighted and grateful to work with Heinemann again. We thank everyone who had a hand (or two) in the production of this book. Special thanks to Vicki Kasabian, who was our production editor; Catrina Swasey and Lynette Winegarner, for editorial coordination and permissions; Kim Cahill, for her deft oversight as marketing manager; Elizabeth Tripp, who taught us quite a few things about copyediting; Suzanne Heiser, our award-winning designer; Sherry Day, skillful filmmaker and zombie portrait maker; and Lauren Audet and her crew for their social marketing acumen. We also appreciate the leadership of Vicki Boyd and Roderick Spellman, twin forces in the world of educational publishing (and overall good human beings). This book needed all of you to bring out the best of our thinking.

WHO IS MAKING THE DECISIONS?

Jillian is halfway through her initial semester, and she feels overmatched by the demands of her university. A mere two months ago she walked confidently into her first college class, but now she is struggling. In high school she completed assignments and projects at the last minute but was skilled enough to turn her mediocre effort into a B average—a sign that indicated she was prepared for college. She is not.

Jillian is studying climate change for a seminar course called Tackling a Wicked Problem. She is expected to research one impact of climate change and to present a recommended course of action. She has a lot of decisions to make: What will be her focus? How can she communicate the urgency of this issue? Should she begin with an anecdote on the impact of rising oceans? How will she set the tone for the piece? How can she most effectively keep her audience (her classmates and anonymous readers of an online magazine) engaged? Is her evidence credible? What order of the evidence is most effective? What are the anticipated counterarguments, and how will she refute them? Jillian is having trouble getting started writing—not because she is lazy or lacks information, but because she has not practiced making these decisions as a writer.

Jillian is surprised—and furious—that teachers in her college courses do not value the five-paragraph essay she has mastered. In high school she didn't have to wrestle with difficult writing decisions, so she chose not to. She was an accomplished follower, a "one draft and done" writer. She determined what the teacher wanted her to say, and *how* the teacher wanted her to say it, and cobbled together thinking she mostly found online. She completed her assignments, but she didn't have to think very hard. Jillian's good grades represented acts of compliance, not decision-making, and now that she's in college, she is beginning to understand what she doesn't know.

Jillian's former teachers had good intentions. They provided structures and step-by-step tasks for students because they had watched young writers struggle or give up entirely, and they wanted to help. Many teachers have concluded that students *can't* write well without detailed instructions.

We disagree.

We believe the detailed instructions are *part of the problem*. Completing teacher-generated step-by-step work is not learning; it masquerades as it. We are reminded of Ellin Keene's research on engagement, where she asks teachers to consider the consequences of their practices: "You may find yourself wondering why you've felt the need to break down tasks into an infinite series of first steps that somehow never add up to the authentic learning experience you'd hoped to create" (Glover and Keene 2015, 108). This thinking echoes the work of Peter Johnston, noted educator and researcher, who adds, "Being told explicitly what to do and how to do it—over and over again—provides the foundation for a different set of feelings about what you can and can't do, and who you are. The interpretation might be that you are the kind of person who cannot figure things out for yourself" (2004, 9).

Which brings us back to Jillian—and to many other students we have encountered who have come to the next step in their education ill equipped to figure things out on their own. They lack practice with doing that difficult work. Many come to believe they are not capable of figuring things out for themselves.

Jillian found she was out of shape when it came to college reading as well. This comes as no surprise to us, as Jillian readily admits she did not read a single book in high school. Jillian did not read books in high school because she didn't have to. All the books were selected by her English teachers—all culled from the traditional, white male canon—and whole-class novel studies lasted weeks and weeks. The thinking she was asked to do had already been done and was easily accessible online. But it would be a mistake to attribute Jillian's lack of reading to her simply having easy access to SparkNotes.

There was another, more important reason. Jillian was not engaged in *reading*; she was bogged down in extended exercises and trying to extract answers. Her teachers assigned chapters to read and then asked her to go find answers buried in the text. Read the chapter. Answer the teacher's questions. Read the next chapter. Answer the teacher's questions. Repeat book after book, year after year. Jillian wasn't making decisions; she was following directions. Worse, the cumulative, numbing effect of this approach over the years began to pull the reins on her love of *all* books.

She is not alone. Many students transfer the negativity of this kind of reading experience and no longer want to read *any* books:

> In 2016, 12th graders reported spending nearly six hours on digital media daily (going online, texting, and using social media). At the same time, their interest in books fell to an all-time low. Sixteen percent of

> 12th-grade students reported reading a book or magazine for pleasure daily in 2016, compared to 60 percent in 1976. (Twenge, Martin and Spitzberg 2018, 11)

Surely no set of standards or skills or the study of a single book is worth what is happening.

Shifting Decision-Making in Our Classrooms

During a book club meeting one night, Penny, Kelly, and Donna Santman, an eighth-grade teacher we both admire, talked over Zoom about the turmoil in our country. Which books felt essential to share with students now? We know that what we bless in our classrooms sends a powerful message to students. All three of us have wrestled with this decision through decades of teaching. At one point, Kelly said, "But some teachers don't have a choice."

Donna jumped in, "*All we do* is make choices. Teachers are always making choices."

Donna's words capture the complexity of teaching. Our daily decisions create a culture of learning in our classrooms. We decide how we care for students. We choose what to say when students tell us they don't read—and they haven't for years. We decide what to do when they share their reluctance to write. How well do we listen to them? The decisions we make in these circumstances have a profound impact.

But here is a bigger question—one that centers this book: *Do the decisions we make enable our students to make decisions without us?* If we choose to teach a new book, for example, but still determine how students will read it, we can't help but funnel them into *our* reading of the book. They will miss the opportunity to bring their experiences to the reading—to see the book like no one else—which would benefit us all. So how do we wean them from the unhealthy codependency that many of them have established with their teachers? How do we lead them to confidence, independence, and joy in reading, writing, thinking, and creating?

That is the work of this book. In four studies we have lifted directly from our classrooms—essay writing, book clubs, poetry, and digital composition—we show you how we work to meet students where they are and hand over much of the decision-making to them. Students need the space to struggle, to wrestle. We aim to build students who can generate a subject of inquiry and stick with it over time. Students who demonstrate the desire to understand and the will to persevere.

Some students will not like this shift—at first. Many of them are content with simply being followers. The road ahead of them has been smoothed; speed bumps have been removed. They quickly learn that the best course of action is to simply stay between the lines. This is problematic, however, as students (like Jillian) are entering a world that will require flexibility. Authors Greg Lukianoff and Jonathan Haidt remind us students will be better off if we "resist the urge to jump in and help them when they are struggling to do things or seem to be doing them the wrong way. Trial and error is a slower but usually better teacher than direct instruction" (2018, 237). Agency and creativity flourish when we give students the space to make decisions, speed bumps and all.

So how do we do this? Let's begin by reimagining how we teach the art of essay writing.

Continuation of credit lines from the copyright page:

Agency *metaphor*

on Community

WILLPOWER

INSPIRATION

Teaching the ESSAY as an Art Form

One of the things we like about our relationship is we often share interesting essays with each other. Recently Kelly sent Penny "I Recommend Eating Chips," a humorous ode to stress eating, by Sam Anderson (2021) of the *New York Times*. Penny sent Kelly a link to The Lives They Lived (*New York Times Magazine* 2020), a rich series of tributes to people lost in 2020. We read essays every day. The subjects are sports, music, politics, love, place, art, life. These essays draw us in; they are varied, descriptive, vibrant. They are real.

And yet, these are not the kind of essays students typically write in secondary schools. Somehow, the literary analysis essay has supplanted all of these rich and varied forms of the essay. Analytic writing is expected to be distant, unemotional, and faceless. Students borrow the thinking of others, imitating the voices of literary critics, and when essay writing becomes a year of writing about one book after another, we never hear *their* voices. We have forgotten that literary analysis is a very narrow slice of what is, in fact, analytical writing. *Analysis* is defined as descriptive, logical, interpretive, inquisitive, organized, orderly, meticulous, searching, exact, precise, accurate, and rational. These words describe personal essays, informative essays, essays of curiosity and wonder, descriptive essays, and, yes, essays that challenge ideas and offer solutions.

To help us recalibrate our thinking, remember the origin of the word *essay*. It comes from the French *essai*, which means "to try or to attempt." Compelling essays are less about certainty and more about exploration. In coming to understand or explore a subject in an essay, the writer should not be bound by form or style. In fact, the writing often increases in power through experimentation with both. Essays should not be standardized; they should offer freedom and possibility. You feel this as you read the opinion pages in your local paper, when you get lost in a compelling blog post, or when you listen to *Modern Love Podcast* episodes. We like what Christina V. Cedillo suggests—that teachers should "transform an essay into an invitational space" (2018).

It is no less analytical to write a comparison of your siblings or friends than to write one of characters in novels. It is no less analytical to interpret a key decision in your life than it is to analyze a key decision in a book. And it is no less analytical to think about your life metaphorically than it is to think about a character metaphorically. Personal essays are not only as rigorous as the traditional school analytical essay but also honor the literacies that diverse students bring to the classroom. Any time we standardize writing, we sideline these diverse voices. Worse, we marginalize them. As Gholdy Muhammad notes in *Cultivating Genius*, it is especially important to give voice to adolescents, who are developing a sense of self:

> Through the developmental years, young people are constantly understanding and (re)making a sense of positive selfhood. This is especially important for culturally and linguistically diverse youth who have a history of being negatively represented and marginalized across large public platforms, including media and schools. To combat this, students need opportunities in class to make sense of their lives so that others cannot tell their stories. (2020, 50)

We cannot tell students their identities matter and then spend the year focused on a soulless form of writing that diminishes the power of their experiences. Historically marginalized students need "urgent pedagogies"—and this urgency is not found by corralling student passion into a template (Muhammad 2020, 54). Our practices can distance students from learning, or they can invite students to use their rich cultural experiences to write with more clarity and power.

When Kieren writes about the effect of the mass murder in his hometown, Sandy Hook, and when Jimena writes about her mother's hardships as a hotel maid, they lean into the writing. They don't begin the writing with an answer; in many cases, it is the writing itself that leads students to insights that surprise them. This writing to understand moves students to analyze again and again. And because these are their stories and no one else's, students must carefully consider the elements of essay writing: how these experiences affect them; how they fit together; what they mean; how the students might organize them; and what voice they should use to compel their readers to listen.

But in order to do this work, we have to be on the same side—the teacher and student, craftsman and apprentice—and the aim must be to produce something of true value. Not to pass a test. Not to prop up a system of comparisons and lies about achievement and intellectual promise. We want students to create a reflection of their lives lived in all their glory and heartbreak, told with honesty and power. We want them ready to share their lived experiences and ideas with others. If we are going to give our students time to write something of value, we have to create conditions that allow them to struggle without penalty. We have to create an approach that counters the unhealthy system of competition that casts such a dark shadow across our students' curiosity and persistence. Writing in this unit is meaningful to the writer, or it is nothing.

To open up the possibilities of essay writing, we will start with Katherine Bomer's definition: "In the electric, pulsating world around us, the essay lives a life of abandon, posing questions, speaking truths, fulfilling a real need humans have to know what other humans think and wonder so we can feel less alone" (2016, ix). That is our work in this unit.

Our Beliefs About Teaching Essay Writing

Belief 1: The five-paragraph essay is a problem now

Because formulaic writing is valued in standardized testing, teachers are in a tough spot. On one hand we want our students to do well when the tests are used as gatekeepers for advancement. Teachers and schools are judged by these scores. Standardized tests still exist as one factor in the admissions process for many colleges and then for scholarships to help pay tuition. Many private schools, charter schools, and even some public high schools use standardized exams to determine who gets in. If that process includes timed essay writing, a formula can help students manage the anxiety with a simplistic structure for their thinking. Students want help passing these tests. We recognize this. But we should also recognize the irony here: although performing well on standardized tests might help students get *into* college, repeated practice of the standardized form makes them ill prepared as writers once they are admitted.

Students are not challenged by five-paragraph-essay (5PE) assignments on books they most often have not read. Writing the same exact essay year after year (and across the curriculum) teaches them that writing is simply labor, not the opportunity to look more closely at the parts of something big and dig deeply to understand them. Formulas have kept them away from real challenges. College freshman composition teacher John Warner argues in *Why They Can't Write: Killing the Five-Paragraph Essay and Other Necessities*,

> Current common approaches for teaching writing are simultaneously too punishing and not nearly challenging enough. Part of the problem is how "rigor" is viewed in education. "Rigor" means "strictness" and "severity." It is an artifact of a different time and a different mentality toward schooling. It remains popular mostly as a way to invoke days

> of yore that are supposedly better than today. . . . When students say a class was "hard," they often mean "confusing" or "arbitrary," rather than stimulating and challenging. (2018, 142)

We would add the following to the list of arbitrary and confusing approaches to teaching writing: rules that demand paragraphs will contain five (or nine or whatever) sentences; the topic sentence will always be first in each paragraph; and the thesis or claim must always be directly stated in the introduction. These rules do not represent excellence in writing. On the contrary: in many cases, adhering to them wrings the goodness out of writing. The writer is punished by being shoehorned into a form. Peter Elbow, noted writing researcher, argues that "the five-paragraph essay tends to function as an anti-perplexity machine" (2012, 308). Katherine Bomer agrees, adding, "There is no room for the untidiness of inquiry or complexity and therefore no energy in the writing" (2016, xi). Not only is energy drained from the writing when students practice mechanized thinking, but students also lose the valuable practice of generating and organizing ideas. When the form is predetermined, much of the writer's important decision-making has already been stripped, which is one reason Penny is now encountering so many college students who believe they cannot solve their own writing problems.

We agree with John Warner's notion that approaches taken by writing teachers are "not nearly challenging enough" (2018, 142). The form does the thinking for the student, and the student simply plugs in and follows. Without an understanding of options, students can't imagine how a different form might better engage an audience or how changing the structure might better communicate their ideas. Teachers in high school rarely (if ever) meet across content areas to consider how often students are writing the exact same formulaic essays. The teachers at our schools never met to have these discussions. Students need numerous opportunities to study the various forms an essay can take, and they need repeated practice experimenting.

This is not our only objection, however. The lack of student decision-making and agency is compounded when students are constrained by the teacher's choice of subject and the lack of an authentic audience for their writing. We like how novelist Lily King explains the problems with standardized essays about books:

> While you're reading [the book] rubs off on you and your mind starts working like that for a while. I love that. That reverberation for me is what is most important about literature. . . . I would want kids to talk and write about how the book makes them feel, what it reminded them of, if it changed their thoughts about anything. . . . Questions like [man

> versus nature] are designed to pull you completely out of the story. . . . Why would you want to pull kids out of the story? You want to push them further in, so they can feel everything the author tried so hard to create for them. (2020, 271)

Beyond the literary essay, consider the ways student voices are amplified today: blogs, podcasts, voice recordings, YouTube videos, TikToks, Instagram stories. Audiences *demand* variation in structure and style. A blog written for skateboarders is going to look and sound different than a TED talk created to explain the coronavirus. But ask yourself how long you would read a blog or listen to a podcast that began like this: "Today, I will discuss *X* and give you three reasons why I believe this to be true."

Please.

We are already dozing off. No one writes like this outside of high school. No one.

How did this mismatch of expectations between what we hope for young writers and what they repeatedly practice happen? We suspect it has a lot to do with the fact that K–12 teachers have too many students, have too little time, and are required to prepare their students for too many mandated standardized tests. In the rush to plan, assess, and respond to the chaos of needs throughout the school day, we have been seduced by a form that is easy to teach and easy to grade.

But let's be honest: we can grade an entire stack of 5PEs without *really* reading them—which might be a good thing, because after closely reading a few of these lifeless essays, we would rather get up and go scrub the bathroom. We understand the very real time pressures put on teachers, but teaching the essay as a vehicle of discovery and understanding does not take any more time. It does, however, take different intentions, different lessons, and new practices to increase feedback to students while they are drafting.

Belief 2: The 5PE is a problem later

One of our mentors, Sheridan Blau, deepened our thinking about how the 5PE is a mismatch for college. Speaking at the University of California, Irvine's Writing Project annual conference in 2019, Blau said: "A university is a knowledge *building* community, and the writing for that community is *an exploration of concerns* within the field of study, a meditation on what a professor is learning, or questions that do not have answers" (italics ours). Blau, who now teaches at Columbia University, reminds us that essay writing is preparation to enter conversations that will occur in class. In addition, the college essay is not a summary of what a text says, but an exploration of how the student responds to the ideas there. Students are expected to put their thinking in dialogue with the ideas of an author and to demonstrate how carefully they have considered that work. College professors expect students to make decisions about organizing their writing and, by the end of the semester, to frame their ideas into five- to ten-page papers exploring questions that lie at the heart of each content area. And they expect this from first-year students.

Penny's college freshmen began their first week of classes feeling (mostly) prepared. They had practiced survival skills in high school to emerge with the grades to get into a university. However, they had invested little of themselves in their writing and, frankly, lacked the experience of developing their own ideas beyond a few paragraphs. These freshmen expected to find assigned topics, templates, and rubrics at their university. They didn't. They were told that the five-paragraph formula they had relied on for success in high school courses was not college-level writing. The students' sense of betrayal (and fear) was real.

Take Jillian, for example. In one course, she was assigned the following: "Identify an idea or challenge in the world (e.g., mass incarceration) and contribute your thinking to readings which will be discussed in class. Respond to the author(s) as you shape your thinking." In Figure 1–1, let's look at the expectations for her research essay alongside the decisions she'd have to make.

There were a lot of big decisions that needed to be made here. This process is not specific to this one assignment, however. We think of another former student, Abby, who was assigned to write four essays on the following topics in her first-year composition course: identity, family, place, and "It was as it shouldn't be." That's it. No additional information or prompts. The students could interpret those ideas in any way. There were no specific guidelines other than each essay had to be at least one thousand words in length. No rubrics. The professor identified great sources of essays but left the students to explore them. The first one was due the next Friday. Go.

Figure 1–2 contains the introductions to three of Abby's essays, each approached differently. We are struck by her voice—how these essays begin by breathing her individuality.

Beyond Abby's introductions, we notice numerous other interesting decisions she makes. In her first essay, she recalls her father's fondness for Joni Mitchell's song "Both Sides Now," and much later in the piece she weaves in some of the song's lyrics in a way that lends the essay a deep poignancy. In her second essay, she weaves in an original poem in the midst of her prose. In her third essay, she begins with a lengthy flashback before transitioning back to the present day. Abby is not writing to adhere to a set of rules put forth by her teacher; she is experimenting with form in search for the best way to say what she wants to say—what she *needs* to say. Her essays vary in length because she's written until she has completed her thinking on a subject.

Expectations for This Research Essay	Decisions Jillian Had to Make
IDEA AND CONTENT	
Develop your thinking about a subject you are curious about; synthesize your analysis of credible sources you find while researching; use the *They Say/I Say* structure to honor the voices of those who have studied your topic, showing the depth of your research and your understanding of the subject.	• What will I focus on? • Which sources am I going to use? • What will be the subideas that I will develop? • Do I have enough research? • What is the best evidence? • Is this author credible?
FORM AND ORGANIZATION	
Hook your readers with a compelling introduction that includes your inquiry question; summarize source material and credit the sources of your information; develop thinking about the claim through subideas and order them most effectively to engage and inform readers; conclude with new insights or challenges to the reader to extend thinking.	• How should I develop my claim? • What form will best convey my thinking? • Where can I find examples of this kind of writing? • What is the best sequence for my ideas or points? • Where should I start? • What transitions between ideas should I use? • How should I conclude?
STYLE	
Use word choice to create a believable, consistent researcher's voice; tune your voice to explain, persuade, and address the reader directly; use literary devices to expertly craft words and sentences; hear the rhythm in your writing.	• Who is my intended audience? • What is my purpose? • Which voice should I use? • How do I achieve this voice? • What is the right word in this spot? • Can I paragraph for effect?
EDITING	
Fine-tune your sentences, balancing long and short sentences for clarity; use a tone appropriate for your intended audience; focus the reader on your central claim; cite sources correctly in the text and in an annotated bibliography of at least five sources; polish your writing by proofreading line by line.	• Have I read my essay out loud? Can I hear it the way I want others to hear it? • Do I have the proper balance of sentence lengths? • Have I spell-checked? Grammar-checked?

Figure 1–1 Research Essay Expectations and Decisions to Make

Essay 1 *(starts with a small moment)*	**Essay 2** *(starts with description)*	**Essay 3** *(starts with a provocative statement)*
"64 Common Pl" the text read as I ran into the half-open elevator. Fluffing my hair into loose brown curls and fidgeting with yesterday's matted face makeup, I attempted to remodel the look of last night. (1,368 words)	Nothing like a summer night in Long Island. It was mid-June, somewhere, on a highway down route 25A toward Mount Sinai. A town forgotten by, but close to Port Jefferson, where there were thousands of tourists. Visiting their families and friends on the edge of the water, because it was so warm outside. Speed-walking, dining, and wearing lavish clothes . . . It seemed they always knew how to smile, even when the ocean breeze cooled the atmosphere. But then dusk would close over the roads, flashing neon yellows, greens, and reds—suddenly, the highways would illuminate. (1,678 words)	On the day your soul died, it was snowing. Snowflakes slowly plummeting toward the surface of a grassy sphere, I walk out my aging door frame and into winter's palest morning. Sneakers sinking into new puddles of fluffy sleet, treading and crunching underneath crushed soles. Murmurs of soft chatter linger in the background of a quiet backyard. I cease in my tracks and blow roasting air into aching fingertips. Sorting through thoughts that always inevitably invade the walls of my mind. (1,430 words)

Figure 1–2 A Writer Experiments with Essay Introductions

Abby believes she learned to write well in two semesters of an elective poetry class in high school. Each of her poems began as an experiment: What's the best way to write about this? There was freedom to play with thinking in her notebook and time to share her fumbling starts with peers. Now in college, her individual sentences ring with expertise:

> Night has fallen and is swirling and twirling around me.
>
> Gold chains hang across his neckline like trophies against a prize.
>
> The fine oil paintings and white pillars line sunken walls. It is a life filled with artificial riches, swishing like change in a pocket of hope. And the noises it made rustled in our dreams.

Abby writes with verve and authenticity. Jillian, the same age, is sitting in a first-year college classroom without the skill set to make the decisions expected of her. And we know this: students get to Abby's level of essay writing when they've experienced a lot of practice in struggling with generating ideas and organizing their thinking. The road to excellence is rife with trial and error. It is up to us to entrust our young writers to wrestle with their decisions. Doing so matters now. And later.

Belief 3: Writing authentic essays embraces playing with form

Essays are less about certainty and more about exploration, and the writer should not be bound by form or style. Take Andrea Gibson's poem, "America, Reloading," in Figure 1–3, for example.

America, Reloading

Andrea Gibson

Mostly because of dying stars,
scientists say space smells like barbecue
and gunpowder. Which is to say
space smells like the United States—

a holiday where we celebrate the independence
of machine guns, how anyone can buy
a cemetery at a sporting goods store
on their 18th birthday

and open carry it to an elementary school
where children are learning tears
don't fall in space. Weightless, without
gravity, they never leave the eye.

Is that what happens to the NRA?
they ask after they've watched the bodies
of half their class use every red crayon
in the universe to scream goodbye.

Do the NRA's tears not drop
because they're astronauts?

How does a parent tell a 6-year-old
that gun sales spike every time
our right to bear massacres
makes a coroner faint,

Makes a mortician say, *I can't,*
my god, I can't.

But we can, can't we, America?
Each election don't we say we can
stomach the boy loading a black hole
into his backpack and unloading it

in the high school hallway
on Valentine's day. It would take
light years to count how many times
the terrified texted I LOVE YOU,

I LOVE YOU, I LOVE YOU
in Parkland, Florida
while the NRA kept crying
in space.

My friend, a second grade teacher,
is instructed to practice hiding her children
in the closet. Twenty-three 7-year-olds
huddle holding their breath.

Holding your breath in space
is the fastest way to die.

The lungs explode in that vacuum
almost as quickly as an AR-15
can make blood-dust
of a closet door.

Of the twenty children murdered at Sandy Hook,
not one of them needed an ambulance.
That's how dead they were.
That's how well the Second Amendment works.

Because there is no air, it is silent in space.
But not as silent as the Christians

continued

on the Senate floor while twenty more families
are asked if they'd like to talk

to a priest. Christ could tear the nails
from his hands and scrape them down
a shrapnel-battered chalkboard
and they'd still be praying for their bank accounts.

After Columbine, parents were notified
about their children in tiny conference rooms.
One family said, *We could hear the family*
before us
screaming, and we knew we were next.

Now loved ones check Facebook
to see who is dead. A mother's status is, *I CAN'T*
REACH MY DAUGHTER. I CAN'T REACH
MY DAUGHTER. Decades after her child
is slaughtered

in the cafeteria
that thought will still be
tearing her from her bed—*I CAN'T*
REACH MY DAUGHTER—

The footprints left by astronauts
on the moon are permanent.
They will never go away
like the grief of a father

identifying his son by his shoes
because the rest of his son's body
was out-lobbied by the NRA, by suits
whispering into the ears of Washington—

This is what we mean
by freedom and justice, the names
of our cities becoming synonymous
with babies being buried

like seeds in the greed gardens of the wealthy.
But you should know your teacher
was a hero, we say. *Her body was found*
bunkering a group of your friends.

And that's as happy as the ending gets
right now. The heroes almost always dead.
The flag at half mass grave.
Children huddled

in basements, trying to tear off their ears
on the Fourth of July because the fireworks
sound like the day everyone died crying,
died with gravity pouring

their next 80 birthdays from their eyes,
while America reloaded,
and moved on
to the next.

Figure 1–3 "America, Reloading," by Andrea Gibson

Yes, this is a poem. *But we also see it as an essay*—albeit in a different form. It is an exploration of the author's rage and sorrow, which could have been written as a traditional essay, but poetry gives it fire. This form—a poem—demands attention. The compression of language builds the explosive power of her ideas. This concentration of details presses a bruise, and the deviation from traditional form surprises us. Gibson uses the literary devices we teach across genres. "America, Reloading" is a story. It is a lament. It is a call to action. It is all of these.

To help our students internalize how forms are blended, we first have them (in pairs or in small groups) surround Gibson's poem and name writing craft moves they notice, much like Kelly's students are doing with an essay in Figure 1–4.

In Figure 1–5, you will see many of the moves they discovered. Because we—their teachers—also did this work on Gibson's poem before class, we are attuned to what they might discover. As they share out observations after close study, we are prepared to nudge them to notice craft moves they may have missed.

The definition of an essay never begins with its form; rather, it is better understood by imagining many forms around one idea. If we use prose to grapple with a big idea, why can't we use poetry or a letter to the editor to do the same thing? We want students to recognize the freedom and power of options, so we invite them to write in other forms that essays take.

Figure 1–4 Students Identify Writing Craft Moves

Writing Craft Moves Noticed by Students in Andrea Gibson's "America, Reloading"

Are italics used to represent thoughts of the writer?

Comparisons (the smell of dying stars to the United States)

Use of capital letters in one place that shows desperation

The stanzas are short. How did she decide this?

Personification: America, reloaded

She plays with language we know in a new way: "a holiday where we celebrate the independence of machine guns."

The spacing made us curious: why are some lines off-set from the rest?

Intentional repetition: I LOVE YOU. I LOVE YOU. I LOVE YOU.

Weaving school shooting with the space metaphor continues start to end.

The length of the lines is not consistent.

Figure 1–5 Craft Moves Students Found in Andrea Gibson's Poem "America, Reloading"

Practices Most Important in Teaching the Essay

What are the skills students need to acquire in order to be independent and creative essay writers? The nine practices listed in this section are not sequential; they are intertwined. We think deeply about how they work together.

Practice 1: We have students generate a volume of ungraded writing

> Freewriting is the easiest way to get words on paper and the best all-around practice in writing that I know. . . . Frequent freewriting exercises help you learn to simply *get on with it* and not be held back by worries about whether these words are good words or the right words.
>
> **—Peter Elbow, "Freewriting"**

Students need a volume of ungraded practice to get comfortable at turning their ideas into words. They also need lessons where they study the organization and style and development of ideas in individual essays. *Writers need both.* Teachers tend to spend more class time analyzing the parts of an essay than giving students time to freely practice responding to a provocative idea, photo, article, poem, or infographic. A volume of ungraded practice gives them opportunities to play with their ideas—some of which they will develop into polished essays using craft moves they learn in this study. We know that the quantity of writing will move more writers toward proficiency. We plan for a balance of both.

Here's an illustration of how quantity leads to quality, taken from *Art & Fear*, by David Bayles and Ted Orland:

> The ceramics teacher announced on opening day that he was dividing the class into two groups. All those on the left side of the studio, he said, would be graded solely on the quantity of work they produced, all those on the right solely on its quality. His procedure was simple: on the final day of class he would bring in his bathroom scales and weigh the work of the "quantity" group: fifty pounds of pots rated an "A," forty pounds a "B," and so on. Those being graded on "quality," however, needed to produce only one pot—albeit a perfect one—to get an "A." Well, came grading time and a curious fact emerged: the works of highest quality were all produced by the group being graded for quantity. It seems that while the "quantity" group was busily churning out piles of work—and learning from their mistakes—the "quality" group had sat theorizing about perfection, and in the end had little more to show for their efforts than grandiose theories and a pile of dead clay. (2014, 29)

This anecdote reminds us of Don Murray, who once said, "The best teacher of writing is the writing." Likewise, in an interview we did with the poet and musician Micah Bournes, he explained that quantity is an essential practice to invite writers to be vulnerable on the page (Gallagher and Kittle 2020b). Using a musician's analogy, he said, "When writing is always performance—no 'skip over tracks'—we are too bound up to write well." We've been there. When faced with writing something important, we need time to try ideas out and discard them before settling on what to include. Kelly wrote many drafts of his mom's eulogy before he got it "right."

When our students were too nervous to post video responses about their reading and writing on Flipgrid, they needed ungraded practice—which was ensured by the Delete key—in order to overcome their fear. They listened to their own responses, judging them by the numerous videos they had watched of people who speak well (in Instagram and Facebook stories or on TikTok). They had internalized criteria for recording an effective video response, and when they felt they didn't meet it, students deleted their responses and tried again. And again. Many confessed to recording and deleting a dozen times before they were satisfied. There is no question that being in control of their practice (in any form of communication) led them to increased proficiency.

We believe we should give students credit for practice. We tell them that measuring quality—their best work—will come at the end of the unit. Throughout the unit we will have lots of practice *that we will begin in class* and encourage them to continue outside of class: in notebook writing, responses to the article of the week, continued work on drafts, and, of course, independent reading, which in itself is an important writing teacher. However, practice is something even published writers resist, so we give our students credit or no credit for their practice both inside and outside of class.

We give credit for total pages written—in words or sketches—in writing notebooks. We ignite the practice in class each day with poetry and other provocations in order for all students to get comfortable with writing. Sometimes they will write a lot about nothing and feel frustrated. All writers do this. Sometimes they will stumble upon language or ideas that surprise them. This brings renewed energy. We hope this "together practice" in class will inspire "alone practice" outside of class. Both are essential. But we recognize that the conditions outside of our classrooms are not fair or equal for all students, so we do not grade students for regular notebook practice outside of class.

We trust in this process, which means that we show students that words beget words beget passions and ideas. We believe that daily quickwrites (thank you, Linda Rief) move writers from *nothing* to *something* better than anything else, and we share some of these later in the chapter.

As adult writers, we are willing to sit and wait for words. Students, however, are often not afforded this luxury. When they are stuck for a long time and are no closer to an idea than they were a few minutes ago, teachers might apply pressure: "Choose something (anything!) and get going." This coercion rarely creates inspiration. When our students say, "I don't know what to write," our reply is, "What you are experiencing is normal for all writers. Start by trying to get some words—any words—on the page. Maybe that writing will help you discover a direction. Relax. Words will come."

Practice 2: We have students look back to move their writing forward

Everyone has curiosities. Quickwrites uncover them. Writers go after things because they are interested in them. They write to answer their own questions. To share their thinking and to invite a conversation with others. Some writing days will feel like wasted time. To counter this, we periodically ask students to reread their notebooks and find threads that run through them. Going back can help a writer move forward. "What patterns do you notice?" we ask. "Is there a quickwrite that calls for more attention?" We demonstrate how we reread our notebooks, highlighting ideas we might want to explore in greater depth.

We have borrowed an exercise from William Stafford, former U.S. poet laureate. In an interview on his writing process, Stafford said, "Each day might start by taking the last phrase you wrote the day before and just taking it farther" (2013, 101). We went back through our notebooks and underlined the last line of each entry. As we underlined, we thought, *Do I have more to say about this?* The answer was often yes. After our students have collected several weeks of daily quickwriting, we ask them to imitate this practice: Underline the last line of each entry. Pick one and copy it down at the top of a new page. Write from that last line for several minutes.

Going back can be just the inspiration needed to move a writer forward.

Practice 3: We project possibilities for how this study of essays might go

We are influenced by Matt Glover and Mary Alice Berry's work (2012) on unit planning: to imagine there are many ways the unit can unfold. They ask teachers to make room for revision of lesson plans and approaches as they lead students in understanding a genre or the process of writing. With their work in mind, here is what we say to students as we launch this unit:

> *Through studying a wide range of essays, you will discover how they are written. We will stand on the shoulders of great writers. In doing so, you might imitate a structure or an author's style. We will use the writing process to polish an essay (written and digitally recorded) that explores an idea, a memory, or a question that is meaningful to you.*
>
> *This is your opportunity to have your say—to share a story that challenges common assumptions or to wonder about the solutions that are possible to a problem. You might explore issues such as racism, the pandemic, or food insecurity. Your essay might be personal (falling in love, or a lesson you learned from siblings or grandparents, or how the storming of the U.S. Capitol impacted your political activism) or it might reach far beyond you (ocean pollution, climate change, homelessness). The world of ideas is open to you.*
>
> *We will be drafting for three weeks. You might settle on an idea quickly and work to polish one draft. Or you might experiment with multiple subjects until you settle on one. Your best draft will be submitted, both as a written essay and as an audio recording.*

Projecting possibilities means we expect some students will struggle to latch onto any topic. We anticipate the inherent differences in how writers work and we plan for time to confer with students and problem solve throughout the unit. We decide on the focus of minilessons *as the unit unfolds.* Our minilessons are not prepackaged because they often arise from student questions and from our observations of what students need to know next. We cannot plan every teaching move ahead of time. We know that our students will struggle at different times and at different places in the writing process.

Practice 4: We launch the unit through text study

We study essays in order to provide students with a vision for writing them. We need a stack of three kinds of essays: published pieces, student essays, and the teacher's model of the process of writing one. We use these texts for minilessons, to facilitate writing group discussions, and occasionally to clarify understanding in a conference.

Collect and study published essays

We give students a packet of eight published essays. We choose a range of styles and moves. These essays (all of which are available online) exhibit different structures:

- a scene (moment in time) that moved to a reflection ("I Fit the Description . . . ," by Steve Locke [2015])
- an analysis that uses pop culture to define roles in society ("Here Be Mother of Dragons," by Maureen Dowd [2019])
- a specific example, which then moves to generalizations ("Sometimes, the Earth Is Cruel," by Leonard Pitts Jr. [2010])
- a generalization, which is followed by a specific, personal example ("The Flags of Our Sons," by Billy Shore [2006])
- a list of evidence, establishing a problem for the reader to solve ("Gamers to the End," by Rick Reilly [2007])
- an anecdote that leads to an idea and then circles back to the anecdote with a deeper understanding ("All Parents Are Cowards," by Michael Christie [2015])
- a list that defines the difference in perspectives ("What the Black Woman Thinks About Women's Lib," by Toni Morrison [1971])
- a story woven into a list of qualities ("Twelve Minutes and a Life," by Mitchell S. Jackson [2020], where he repeats the phrase "he was more than . . ." to describe Ahmaud Arbery)
- the use of an extended metaphor ("The Colors of His Addiction," by Lauren Mauldin [2019])

On the first day, we read one of the essays together and have the students discuss what they notice. On the second day, we read a different essay and ask them if this one is better than the first one. There is no best, but comparing sharpens their attention to the craft moves in each piece as they defend their choices. Over the next few days, they read the remaining essays and rank them one through eight, from most to least engaging. We ask students to revisit the essays to highlight why they found some more intellectually challenging or enlightening than others. These opening days allow us *with* students to create the criteria for excellence in essays (see "Assessment and Grading" on page 37). Our goal, we tell them, is to understand the possibilities in both ideas and craft moves that make essays fascinating, memorable, and worth reading again.

Students work in writing groups to share their observations of these essays. Class ends with each group sharing notes. Students will likely identify how the author explains or develops a big idea and responds to it, how the writer weaves in facts and references (both historical and popular or current), how a compelling voice makes the topic more meaningful, and how the use of literary devices adds nuance and sophistication to the rhythm of the writing. When students are identifying craft moves, we encourage them to be both specific (e.g., the essay begins with an anecdote) and general (e.g., all essays do this . . .). Although some of these published essays demonstrate craft that is far beyond the capabilities of our students, we want to show them what is possible.

Here are other places you might find well-written essays: The *New York Times Magazine* Lives column ran from 1996 to 2017 and is still available online. This is a series of incisive, eight-hundred-word essays that highlight small moments in people's lives. Titles range from "The Cat Named Morphine" to "This Cold House." We also spend time with the This I Believe essay collection (https://thisibelieve.org), which is subtitled, "A Public Dialogue About Belief—One Essay at a Time." The titles on this site range from "Always Go to the Funeral" to "Be Cool to the Pizza Dude." In other words, anything goes.

Collect and study student essays

We study essays from former students that show insight, courage, and humor. We choose a stack of texts written by former students because they have skill sets similar to the students that sit before us. We don't want all of our mentor texts to be too far out of reach for writers who are new to finding their voice and direction in a subject of their choosing. As Sheridan Blau says, "the best person to help you is one step ahead of you" (2019).

We keep copies of student essays each year that we find compelling. With the students' permission, we share these (without the students' names to protect their privacy). We label these PSU 2021, for example, or put a short note about the student (three-sport athlete, now studying psychology at UNE). Penny collected twenty-five student essays and copied them into packets that she left at the center of each table throughout this unit. Her high school students who were stuck could refer to them for inspiration. Some students read these during independent reading. Every few years she updates this collection. In her classroom library there are at least ten years' worth of these packets available.

If this approach to teaching the essay is new to you, consider the collection of eight personal essays (out of eight thousand entries) that won the *New York Times* personal narrative essay contest in 2019. The *Times* Learning Network explained, "[We] challenged teenagers to write short, powerful stories about meaningful life experiences. . . . Beyond a caution to write no more than 600 words, our rules were fairly open-ended, and we weren't sure what we would get" (Learning Network 2020). Each of the eight published essays could be used to launch this unit. Other excellent resources include *Teen Ink* and *Teen Vogue.*

Study the teacher's model of process

Beyond published essays and student essays, there is a third essential model in our stack: pieces we write alongside our students. Our *emerging* essays are a model of process, not product. The teacher is an essential bridge between the chaos students feel when asked to organize their ideas and the finished products we have been studying together. It is up to us to show them how we navigate the decisions as we move from idea to draft.

We might print our rough draft and ask students to read and comment on it, or we might use our draft to anchor a minilesson where we demonstrate more than one way to organize our ideas. Throughout the unit this process unfolds as we model the decisions writers wrestle with. This includes finding a subject in our notebook, deciding on a style to effectively move an audience, and how to ask for feedback to help us improve our writing.

We confess, though, that we don't always write an original essay each year. Sometimes we tell students we want to revisit a draft we worked on prior to this unit. Sometimes we start a draft in one class and stay with it in subsequent classes.

Practice 5: We lead the study of essays from whole to parts

We plan the study of a genre with four kinds of text-study lessons. Teachers who use mentor texts sometimes get distracted by details of craft, as we admit we do, without seeing the essay as a whole. We can be more purposeful about our teaching when we understand how the building blocks of essays are constructed. This is big-picture thinking, and it leads students to deeper understandings of the decisions they must make about the organization of their ideas. We discuss these examples in the order that we believe is essential to understand the *whole* of an essay.

1. ***Vision* generates options.** When our students are thinking about possible subjects, we want them to consider both topic and organization. Essays are written about experiences that taught us, formed us, or challenged us. We also select essays that have distinctly different structures. We seek to develop a key understanding: a writer *chooses how* to write about a subject. The writer might take a "small" approach, as Steve Locke did in "I Fit the Description . . .," where he describes a moment when he was detained by the police (2015). This is different from the "big" approach Michael Christie takes in "All Parents Are Cowards" (2015), where he looks at the effect of his agoraphobic mother on the course of his life. Here is another possibility: give students models of the college admissions essay. We chose ones that resulted in admission to elite colleges. All excellent, all different. (One student wrote about shopping in Costco and another wrote about financial instability over the course of his life.) Our students work to name the characteristics of their different structures, so that we can collectively create a vision for possibility within this form.

2. ***Order* creates momentum.** The writer must determine the most effective shape to transmit their idea. The way paragraphs are ordered creates momentum and the shape of the whole. The writer makes lots of decisions: Where do I slow down the reader to focus on something important? What parts can I condense? Speed past? Do I want this essay to build to a crescendo or begin at the resolution of a crisis and use flashbacks? The focus of our study is to help students play with the most effective sequence. The language we use with students (both in minilessons and in conferences) might go like this: "Once you have storyboarded the chunks of your essay, reconsider your sequence. What would your essay look like if you started here instead of there? Is this the best beginning? Or would it be best to move this to the end of the essay?"

3. ***Style* communicates point of view.** The point of view is established in the examples or evidence the writer selects. (For example, Penny could write an essay based on the claim that her father was the most generous man she knew and include moments when he demonstrated it. Or she could write about her father's alcoholism and the impact it had on her family.) The voice will change based on the writer's purpose. There are many voices inside each of us, and voice begins at the word level. It creates the tone (the author's attitude toward the subject) and also communicates mood (the way we want readers to feel as they read). Words create humor or contemplation, heartache or joy. We lead students to identify the writer's style by analyzing these choices.

4. ***Sentences* create rhythm.** It is important for students to pay attention to the art of the sentence. Sentences are composed with a balance between long and brief streams of words. They contain literary devices like alliteration and metaphor. When we study texts at the sentence level, we name, notice, and share the beauty of both elegant and simplistic construction. We note when authors break sentence rules (e.g., intentional fragments or run-ons). We look at how sentences compose paragraphs. We study the way sentence parts contribute to the whole of the essay, considering how the structure of a single sentence or paragraph adds meaning.

These four ways of studying essays are built upon lessons we teach throughout the year. We connect our lessons about writing across genres regularly so that students have a continuous line of thinking to hang new ideas on. A student who learned how to write an anecdote in a narrative unit and then weaves an anecdote into their current argument piece understands the use of that craft move beyond their initial understanding or application of the skill. Two important things are happening here: the student practices using a skill again, and when practicing this skill in a different genre, they improve their craft. Same skill. Wider application.

Practice 6: We teach students to choose a form

When a writer chooses the form (e.g., time line, letter, circle, definition, compare and contrast, cause and effect), the writer must first understand how that form contributes to meaning. Take the writer Ta-Nehisi Coates, for example. His National Book Award–winning nonfiction book, *Between the World and Me* (2017), is a letter to his teenage son on how to navigate a world rife with racism. Because it is written in letter form, it has a personal, intimate feel. However, Coates also wrote a feature article for *The Atlantic*, "The Case for Reparations" (2014), a multigenre ten-segment piece in which he strings together anecdotes, maps, video, photographs, letters, and primary source documents to make his case. This stacking of evidence gives the piece authority. In both examples, it's not just the words that make his case; *it is the form*.

This is a decision we want all our students to consider: which form of the essay will best connect their writing to readers? Understanding the power of form begins with studying alternative options. We introduce our students to the idea of a circle essay, which begins with an anecdote, then comes back to the same scene at the end. We model the shape and structure of powerful cause-and-effect essays, like Mitchell Jackson's "Twelve Minutes and a Life" (2020), which traces events that led to the death of Ahmaud Arbery. Once students can experiment with the many forms of the essay, they are positioned to consider possibilities for their own essays.

Here are five other possibilities.

The narrative essay: The writer tells a story or puts together one or more moments that illustrate a unifying idea. The writer answers the question, "Why does this matter?" Or the writer might make a claim about something observed to be true and then illustrate that truth by referring to events and situations that the writer has experienced.

The graphic essay: The writer combines sketches and words. We introduce this with a contemporary collection of mentor texts from "Art in Isolation: An Ongoing Visual Diary in Our Uncertain Times," by the *New York Times* (2020).

Students determine how they will work in this mode. Some will create graphic essays. For Spencer, the act of sketching (see Figure 1–6) led him to memories and words. Rough-draft storyboard sketches helped him to decide on the most powerful images to use and how they might be sequenced. Spencer's graphic essay could be used as a springboard to write a narrative essay with more depth than he might have otherwise.

Figure 1–6 Spencer's Storyboard for a Graphic Essay

Ekphrasis, or the essay as an examination of art: Ekphrasis is defined as a literary description of or commentary on a visual work of art. Writing next to art can guide students toward imaginative writing when studying narrative. We can imagine the subjects as characters in a drama we create on the page. Both of us have used Kehinde Wiley paintings for this purpose. This question from Sylvan Barnet's *A Short Guide to Writing About Art* is a helpful guide:

> What do the clothing, furnishings, accessories (horses, swords, dogs, clocks, business ledgers and so forth), background, angle of the head or posture of the head and body, direction of the gaze, and facial expression contribute to our sense of the figure's social identity (monarch, clergyman, trophy wife) and personality (intense, cool, inviting)? (2018 study guide)

Writing about art takes students deeper into the art itself. It supercharges noticing and analysis skills. Adapted from Barnet, here are possible approaches to story writing that we could model:

- Write as the characters in the artwork speaking to the viewer.
- Write about the scene you see in the artwork.

- Think about what the subjects did after the painting.
- Write a conversation between the characters in the piece.

After imagining our way into the painting's details, we ask students to share which details they noticed and how that impacted their stories of the work. We are walking them into the work of writing essays *on the work* by quickwriting stories in notebooks.

As we move to essay writing about art, we select one provocative photograph found in What's Going on in This Picture?, a Learning Network feature of the *New York Times*. We quickwrite captions to the photograph. Students can submit their captions in the comments section and read hundreds of student examples there as well. Captions tell about a photograph, a different form of writing than creating a story of the photograph.

Here are two examples of writing a few sentences next to a photograph to demonstrate the difference for students. Notice the differences (tone, information, word choice) demonstrated in the two captions in Figure 1–7.

Likewise, we model composing commentary (as with the picture of Kelly and his daughter) as we study a painting, like Brian Collier's *He Who Watches Over Israel* (see Figure 1–8).

Story: Kelly and his daughter, Caitlin, attend game six of the 2017 World Series in Los Angeles. It was Caitlin's dream to see her beloved Dodgers play in a world series. The Dodgers won this tense game, beating Justin Verlander and the Houston Astros by the score of 3–1. It is a memory that Kelly and Caitlin still cherish.

Commentary: Kelly and his daughter, Caitlin, attend game six of the 2017 World Series in Los Angeles. Although the Astros won the championship the next night, it was later revealed that they had participated in a cheating scheme that provided their batters with an unfair advantage. As a result, Major League Baseball should have stripped the Astros of their title. The fact that they didn't is shameful.

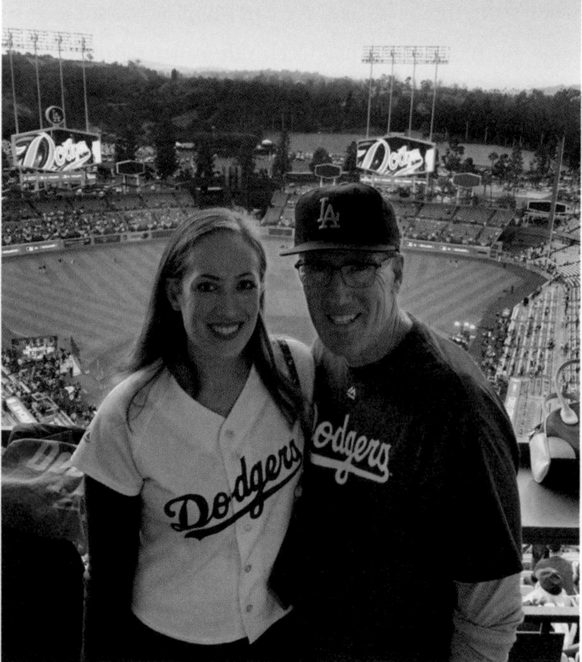

Figure 1–7 Two Ways to Write About a Photograph

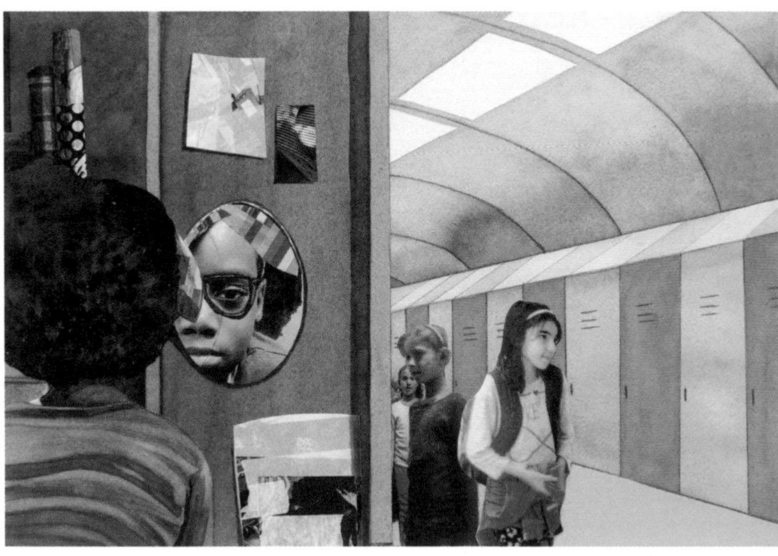

Figure 1–8
He Who Watches Over Israel, by Bryan Collier

Here are possible approaches, adapted from Barnet, to writing commentary on this painting that we could model:

- Write about your emotional response to the artwork.
- What does this work of art say to you?
- Imagine what Collier intended for this piece.

In both these approaches, students will be led deeper into the art itself. We like that these questions do not have right answers and do lead to expansive thinking and writing. Students select a work of art to study—a painting, sculpture, or photograph—and begin this process of analysis. They will reflect both on what they see and what they think the work of art means.

The digital essay: Often, one can elevate an essay in written form by turning it into a digital form. All major events in history, from the murder of George Floyd to the siege on our nation's capitol, are produced as digital texts by major media outlets. (For example, see "The Crackdown Before Trump's Photo Op," by Bennett et al. [2020].) These short movies mix the written word with video clips, newscast footage, photographs, and maps. These compositions are every bit as complex as written essays, and this mash-up of media has an undeniable power. We expect our students to compose digital texts, and current examples provide powerful models for their texts. We delve deeper into digital composition in Chapter 4.

The multigenre essay: In *Revolution*, Deborah Wiles (2017) mixes fiction and nonfiction imagery and artifacts to tell the story of the turbulent 1960s in America. In *Kent State* (2020), she mixes poetry and prose to recall the horrific events of May 4, 1970. Her blending of genres and imagery is powerful storytelling.

Kelly had his students do a number of quickwrites after studying poems, art, photographs, charts, and articles when the pandemic thrust his students into distance learning. At the end of the unit, he asked them to revisit their quickwrites and to find one to turn into an essay. Ahmed created a multigenre essay that included the following elements:

- ten ways—with detailed explanations—on how to stay safe
- a dispelling of two key conspiracy rumors
- an analysis of graphs and charts about flattening the curve and the spread of the virus to world hot spots
- a firsthand account of witnessing panic and hoarding at the grocery store, woven around photographs he had taken of barren shelves and long lines

Together, this tapestry of pieces gives the reader a deeper understanding of the early days of the pandemic—much more so than one essay or story alone could have done. For more on multigenre writing, we recommend Tom Romano's *Blending Genre, Altering Style* (2000).

You might think these six examples—Andrea Gibson's poem essay, the narrative essay, the graphic essay, the ekphrasis essay, digital composition, and the multigenre essay—are far from the standard definition of essay writing, and you are right. But in fact, composition is composition. We are teaching students to compose. In all of these examples, students must make decisions about content, audience, approach, clarity, and cohesiveness.

As Tom Newkirk, former director of first-year composition for the University of New Hampshire, said in an editorial conversation about this book, "Writing is a form of action: it's not what writing *has*; it is what writing *does*. Genre should be a generative thing, not a limiting thing." Certainly "the five-paragraph-you-know-what," as Romano famously called it (2004, 60), does one thing well: it limits the range of writers. This is not what we want. On the contrary, to ignite a passion for writing in our students, we must expand the form of the essay.

The forms of writing will change across time. Any list of essay possibilities that we print here might be outdated by the time you read this. Consider how zines and TikTok value brevity while posts on Longreads value extended exposition and complexity. We can prepare our current students for only one thing: to imagine options. Lin-Manuel Miranda read the nonfiction biography *Alexander Hamilton*, by Ron Chernow, and envisioned a hip-hop mixtape. He understood that possibility. We couldn't. We had listened to hip-hop but never written it.

How can we tap into our students' curiosity with composition? A biography might inspire a poem. A song might inspire a digital commentary. A painting might inspire an argument. If our students are blind to these and other options, we have stunted their creative meaning-making potential.

We are cautious here. We do not believe that every student needs to write each of these forms. Rather, writers need to understand their options and make choices about the forms that fit their subjects, purposes, and audiences. *I choose this form* orients the writer to the act of composing differently than *I will practice this form that was chosen for me*. Again we ask: Who is making the decisions?

Practice 7: We lead students to read, analyze, and imitate passages

We want our students to learn from other writers, so we often select passages for close study. We practice three skills:

Read. (What does this passage say?)

Analyze. (What are the writerly moves in the passage?)

Imitate. (What did this writer do that I can do?)

Remember, first we study essays at the *whole-text level* (practice 5), where we identify the use of patterns and forms as possible ways to structure their thinking. When we shift to the study of *parts* or passages, we ask students to imitate sentence patterns.

It is through the act of imitation that young writers get to try on the moves of other writers. For example, Figure 1–9 shows the last three paragraphs of Gail Caldwell's "Learning How to Love from Afar" (2020), which captures the struggles of living in a pandemic. Kelly and Penny modeled imitations of this for students in different ways. Notice in bold where Kelly used Caldwell's phrases to gain momentum in his writing.

We encourage this level of in-class plagiarism. We recognize that the word *plagiarism* is from the Latin *plagiarius*, which translates to "kidnapper." We often kidnap the structure and patterns other writers use in order to create momentum in notebook practice. We remind our students, however, that if we were to publish a piece that imitated another writer's work this closely, we would have to cite the source of our inspiration.

We also hope that some students will create their own structure after reading the mentor text. Penny attempted a side-by-side imitation like Kelly's in her notebook but then abandoned

Final Paragraphs of Gail Caldwell's "Learning How to Love from Afar"	Kelly's Imitation
My neighbors and I have driveway parties **where we** line up lawn chairs for the four of us, 10 feet apart, and laugh about nothing. One night I take over a pot of chicken soup; two days later a friend of a friend brings me a roaster she found at the store. We start to call it the chicken cycle of life.	Every Wednesday night, my lunch table buddies meet on Zoom, **where we** drink and play Quiplash and Joke Boat online, a closeness from miles apart, a small window of chance to laugh our way through the solemnity of the times. A standing weekly lifeline.
I'd been making a maypole, adorned with ribbons, from old bamboo stakes for the front yard, but today it seems like a dumb idea; today, bleakness has beat out perseverance.	**I'd been** working in my notebook capturing this moment in history, replete with news stories, photographs, quotations, and reflections—a way of wrapping my mind around the history unfolding around us. It seems like a good idea, but yesterday the bleakness of it all caught up with me.
Then my adored 10-year-old friend comes crashing down the driveway, stopping the bike halfway to me. I gasp in happiness. "I miss you so much," I cry, and Tyler cries back, "I miss you too!" Together we put our arms up and out, heart surfing, bending toward each other like reeds. We have learned, lickety-split, how to love one another from afar.	**Then my** daughter's face popped up in Facetime on my phone, stopping my depression in its tracks. I gasped in happiness, "I am so happy to see you," my voice choking up. "I am happy to see you, too, Dad." Together, we discuss her new life—moving into a new place with her boyfriend, the marriage proposal hiding just around the corner. I hear the love in her voice—her happiness—and, suddenly, I realize just how fortunate I am.

Figure 1–9 Three Paragraphs of Original Writing and Kelly's Imitation

the first two parts and focused only on the last paragraph, where she found inspiration. This focus launched her to write a scene:

> Today on a trail in the woods I heard a voice calling, "Penny! Ms. Kittle!" and I saw my son's childhood best friend and his huge yellow lab bounding toward me.
>
> "Ryan!"
>
> "I knew that was you!" His smile blinked between sunshine and shade. His voice. His eyes. It was all so familiar. I saw Cam walking out of his elementary school two days after we moved here, yelling, "Mom, I met a friend," as Ryan stepped shyly to my car window. I see the two of them in hockey practice, side by side at the net or racing down the ice, then hugging wildly as Cam scored a hat trick on his birthday. I see them bent over notebooks in my class senior year, then on prom

night, at graduation, at Cam's wedding. Ryan flew in from Seattle to hold Cam's new daughter so carefully; both of them were again two young boys filled with wonder. Could it have just been last summer that Ryan's band stopped to play nearby and we all went to hear them in a barn?

Maisie danced. We celebrated a purple sunset.

Ryan handed me a history of riches in his grin this morning. And I remembered: gratitude trumps fear.

Pay attention.

We're still living here.

As she wrote this, Penny began to imagine this as a digital story. She saw the photographs in her head that would accompany the history of this moment. She envisioned reading the words above as a voice-over that would accompany these images. What started as imitation practice became a form that was not initially considered. Motivated by possibility, she spent hours creating a tribute to best friends that she eventually shared with them on her YouTube channel. Penny could imagine her writing as a digital composition simply because this option lived inside her. We want our students to imagine this option as well.

Practice 8: We move writers forward with writing conferences and writing groups

Talk improves writing. We often can't see the holes and rabbit trails in our own writing; when read aloud, the writing gets better for two reasons. One, we hear writing read aloud. And two, someone else hears it and gives us feedback. As we were writing this paragraph, for example, we revised it numerous times as we read it aloud to one another. Penny suggested a cut, and Kelly suggested a rearrangement. We have to hear how our ideas support one another in a paragraph in order to see if our writing matches our intent. We are on the lookout for how examples we use improve clarity overall. If we recognize the value talk plays in improving our writing, we also have to recognize how valuable talk is for young writers. This talk occurs in both one-on-one conferences and writing groups. Let's take a look at these practices.

One-on-one conferences

We sit beside writers every day in our classrooms. This fundamentally shifts our understanding of teaching and learning in each unit. Until you set up a system to make this happen regularly, you will never gain the insight you need to become the best writing teacher you can be.

Our purpose with conferences is to coach, not to criticize. This is an important distinction. We are looking for strengths in their writing, and we begin our conferences by reinforcing them. As Buckingham and Goodall note,

> learning is less a function of adding something that isn't there than it is of recognizing, reinforcing, and refining what already is. . . . Neurologically each brain grows where it is already strongest. Getting attention to our strengths from others catalyzes learning, whereas attention to our weaknesses smothers it. (2019)

This is worth repeating: *focusing on strengths catalyzes learning; focusing on weaknesses smothers it.* Therefore, we use language in these conferences intentionally to encourage and propel writers. Students are often unaware of the power in their writing. Buckingham and Goodall suggest that the words we choose help students to see their strengths:

> Use phrases such as "This is how that came across for me" or "This is what that made me think," or even just "Did you see what you did there?" Those are your reactions—they are your truth—and when you relay them in specific detail, you aren't judging or rating or fixing him; you're simply reflecting to him the unique "dent" he just made in the world, as seen through your eyes. And precisely because it isn't a judgment or a rating it is at once more humble and more powerful. (2019)

In a *Washington Post* interview, Buckingham (2019) asks us to think about these conversations as "strengths replays." He adds, "The best sports coaches record the winning plays in each game and say, 'This is what excellence looks like for you.'" Strengths replays should be a part of every writing teacher's playbook.

And yet, sometimes these midprocess conferences tell us we are out of touch with our students—that our coaching is not even in the right ballpark. Kelly, for example, conducted a whole-class lesson on writing introductions, and then he circulated the room to help students as they drafted them. He sidled up to Anton, who was staring at a blank page in his notebook. Kelly asked him if he had thoughts about how he might start his essay. Anton hemmed and hawed; a couple of minutes into the conference, Kelly realized Anton didn't have enough information to begin envisioning his piece, so the minilesson Kelly taught was premature. If Kelly had begun by asking, "What can I help you with, Anton?" he would have been honoring Anton's decision-making. *The writer should determine the focus of a conference.*

Often in conferences, we use "writing in the air," a strategy Katie Wood Ray named, to help a writer get started, or to imagine a next move middraft, or even to talk through ways to end the piece. This talk helps the writer get feedback on the clarity of their ideas *as they write*. Here's an example of the use of this strategy in Penny's class:

> **Penny:** Hey, Spencer, what's happening in writing today? What are you working on?
>
> **Spencer:** I'm writing about my car.
>
> **Penny:** Why?
>
> **Spencer:** Because I love it.
>
> **Penny:** What do you love about it?
>
> **Spencer:** It's rare.
>
> **Penny** (*Waits for more.*)
>
> **Spencer:** No one has one.
>
> **Penny** (*Waits for more.*)
>
> **Spencer:** It makes me think about my mom. . . . Oh, you're *good*! You didn't do nothing! You just sat there and pulled this out of me!
>
> **Penny** (*Smiles.*)
>
> **Spencer:** The car was my mom's and now that she's gone, I feel closer to her driving it.
>
> **Penny:** Well, I'm done here. You know what you're trying to say.

This conference was less than two minutes long, but it helped Spencer identify what was missing in his writing. This could not have been accomplished by walking around the room to keep them all on task. We understand the urge to hover. We want to control the room. We stretch our energy out across a sea of students to keep them in line, often ignoring those who are working, while we zoom in on those who we suspect are wasting time. But hovering does not move writers.

Here's an example of the difference: Penny observed a sixth-grade classroom where the teacher gave the students twenty-five minutes to work on their writing. During that writing time, the teacher paced up and down the rows in order to check on lots of students—"How are you doing? OK? Keep going." Although she was well intentioned, her movement and talk were distractions.

As long as we hover, we see writers only through the lens of managing them. But when we get close to a young writer, we see through the lens of learning. We become researchers—and yes, we can still manage the classroom. We teach our students that they can work independently while we work with students individually. We believe they can solve many of their own problems. If we glance up and sweep the room while crouched beside a student, we might decide to go next to a student who we think is wasting time and distracting others. We might. We might not. We could save that conversation for later since it will likely distract those nearby.

Penny moved to sit beside one boy in that teacher's class. Although he was following the teacher's directions, he had not considered his ending. Penny talked with him briefly about possibilities before moving to sit by a girl nearby. She was revising her draft, thinking it was finished, but had stopped working because she was listening to Penny's conference. She was now reconsidering her ending. And of course, that is the power of these small moments with writers—they multiply thinking in the room because students are naturally curious about what we say to other students. When Penny stepped away from this second conference, she scanned the other students in the room. How many had not planned their endings? Suddenly, she was thinking like a researcher: determining what to teach next. This is the *work* of teaching.

We imagine this prepared and enthusiastic young teacher had included the importance of a conclusion in her directions and perhaps even highlighted some in mentor texts at the start of the unit. It isn't that the teacher didn't know the importance of endings, but knowing *when* to teach something matters as well. Young writers find it hard to retain information when they are not in position to receive it. With all of the concerns writers have to get started and to gain momentum into their writing, considering how to end a piece can easily be cast aside. Students forget you modeled it three days ago. We need to know more about our students *in real time* so that we can plan for our teaching to be most effective. How many students are ready—right now—for a lesson on endings? The answer to that question will lead us to either small-group coaching or a whole-class minilesson.

That minilesson might go like this:

I'm going to ask you to imagine your ending before you've written the rest of your draft. Now that you're well into your draft, you have a sense for where it is going and where you want to take your readers. The practice of looking ahead to your ending is sometimes a helpful part of your writing process. You don't have to commit to an ending, but when you consider your options, it can lead you to write the rest of your draft with greater purpose and drive.

We would then teach possibilities through examples of endings from mentor texts. The teaching of options at this stage of their work invites students to be problem solvers as they work.

Management matters. Systems matter. But only if they free you and your students to do better work in that space—the learning work. The wrestling work. The questioning and problem-solving work for both students and teachers. This is one reason we make conferring a natural, everyday practice in our classrooms. And doing so reminds us that every minute spent hovering is a lost minute of personalized instructional time.

Writing groups

Though we know that midprocess conferring with each writer is the most effective way to elevate student writing, we are faced with an unforgiving reality: we can't get to every writer when they need us. There are too many students and not enough time (Kelly's classes averaged thirty-eight students). Because of this, we must help our students to provide meaningful feedback to one another. We have found the most effective way of doing this is to place our students into small writing groups.

Writing groups, however, are not to be confused with peer editing groups. We do not put students into groups to edit each other's drafts. We have two issues with this practice. One, our students' developing understanding of grammar and sentence structure is often not strong. They make incorrect edits on their peers' drafts, or simply say, "It looks good to me," and nothing is gained for either writer. And two, when students believe the mission of reading someone else's draft is limited to finding mistakes, they develop a tunnel vision that doesn't address the bigger issues of the piece. Too many students clean up their own rough drafts instead of diving deeper into the content of them. "Is my comma in the right place?" is not the same conversation as "What do you know about my brother after reading this scene?" We want students hungry to communicate well, not just edit. We seek to build a community where students work through questions and hesitations as they write together. Who cares if the piece is flawlessly edited if the essay is underdeveloped and lifeless?

While we have both created writing groups in our classrooms for years, we found engagement increased when we also connected our students across the country. Our students were energized when given the opportunity to interact meaningfully with students from other cultures and backgrounds. We placed them in groups of six—three students from Kelly's classes grouped with three students from Penny's classes. We not only asked the students to share their drafts within these small groups but required them to ask for targeted responses on Flipgrid from their group members.

What do we mean by targeted responses? We have all had students come up to us, plop their drafts down, and simply ask, "Can you help me?" This is an act of learned helplessness—an example of young writers ceding the decision-making process to the teacher. Students must move beyond this. We require them to ask others in their writing group for *specific* feedback on their drafts. To model what this looks like, we go first. For example, our Flipgrid requests were as follows:

> **Kelly:** *Thanks for agreeing to take a look at my paper. There are two things I'd like you to look at. The first is the part when I yell "Stop!" and the same moment my mom yells, "Stop!" I don't know—it feels kind of clunky and awkward in there. So, I am wondering if that part works for you as a reader. The other thing is that there are three different times in the piece where I say my dad and I locked eyes with one another. This was intentional repetition. I'm wondering if that resonated with you. Was it forced? Was it lame? Or did it work? Did you even notice it? So could you please take a look at that?*
>
> **Penny:** *I am hoping you might answer one question. This piece is mostly about how much I loved spending time with my dad, and yet I feel like the whole first section is so dark that it doesn't offer enough light after that—I mean, really, the thing with him coming to my tennis match does not paint him as very involved . . . and it's not really until the bottom of page 2 and the start of page 3 where I start getting into what, to me, really matters. So, I feel like my balance is off. Can you just comment on what you think about that? Thanks.*

We modeled two different ways to ask for a response. Kelly's was specific to two moments in his piece, while Penny's was about how the scenes she'd chosen contributed to an understanding of her relationship with her father over time. Kelly and Penny responded to each other's requests, and our students responded to our drafts as well. Then it was their turn.

Here is Alyssa asking her writing group for feedback:

> I need some advice about the ending. I feel as though I rushed it a bit. I spent a lot of time explaining the first part and the ending is kind of just like—Bam!—this happened and bye. So let me know what you think.

From across the country, Noelia responded:

> The conclusion—I think—I'd love your conclusion if it only ended when you said that you were out like a light. Because when you said you were "appendix-less," I feel like we know that you are going into the surgery, but when you end with "I went out like a light" it creates some suspense. So I think it would be better if you ended it like that . . . it can create the reader to say, "Wow, she's getting the surgery." And it leaves us in suspense to ask what happened next.

This is only one response that Alyssa received. Now imagine the value she got from other writers in her group. And this value was soon multiplied, as Alyssa then read five other students' essays in her group and responded to each of *their* questions. She had to swim in the writing of other students, which exposed her to all kinds of writerly moves that may have ended up influencing her own draft. And all of this reading and responding comes with a bonus: students learn that the *writer* should determine the focus of the response.

Outside of writing groups, we reinforce this. No draft is accepted by the teacher unless the writer has asked a question that provides the teacher with a lens to read the draft. A student might ask, "Do my transitions work?" or "Do I have enough evidence to support this position?"

We would also like to note that the value of peer response extends beyond midprocess response. We had students respond to one another in the prewriting stage as well. Christian was having trouble deciding how to focus his research, so he posted a pitch on the class Flipgrid page and asked for response (see Figure 1–10).

Figure 1–10 Screenshot from Christian's Flipgrid

My research topic is on the Queen Mary*—the boat in California. My main topic is if the haunting stories are real. And then I just have my subtopics. I have a few that just kick off with the main one. So I have, When and where did the ship come from? The whole history of the ship being haunted, what was its main purpose and use when it was originally built? Why was it made into a hotel? And then I have some other subtopics—like I want to do research on Ouija boards. I just want to know everything about them, really . . . everything we can know. I want to do research on who made the Top Ten Most Haunted*

Places ever. I want to know how they decide that. Because they just say it and they don't really explain, like they give a description of all the things that were haunted there. They don't say why this one is this, or they don't say why it is more haunted than other ones. I want to figure out why it is like that. And that's really it for now. I'm hoping you guys can give me some ideas that are better than the ones I have. Thank you.

Christian's thinking, like that of many students early in the writing process, is all over the place. Should he write about the *Queen Mary*? The ten most haunted places ever? Ouija boards? We want to help each one of these students, but a teacher's time is limited. When students ask other students for ideas, it can help them get started. Joseph posted a reply (see Figure 1–11).

Figure 1–11 Screenshot from Joseph's Flipgrid

In regards to your search optic on the Queen Mary, *and whether or not it is haunted, I actually have a friend who went there this past weekend and she told me about how she heard clanking of pipes in the distance. That could just be sound effects. She also saw that when she took a picture, the face of a ghost showed up. And so, nowadays with technology, it raises the question on whether or not the* Queen Mary *does this for the tourists and for the money, or whether or not it is actually real. So you can do more research on that to find out if it is actually legitimate or not.*

Joseph's response ignored much of Christian's musings and zeroed in on one element: Is the haunting actually real? Christian started researching that and came to Penny's office having been up all night following this thread. He was intrigued and fascinated. He angled all of his research in this direction.

Writing groups do more than give students feedback on their work. They create community.

Practice 9: We turn decisions over to students

Following are key decisions students should make over the course of this unit, along with the language we use in the classroom.

Choose a subject:

You will develop your own topics. Often, your essays will spin out of your quickwrites, but you are free to look anywhere for inspiration. We are not all writing the same essay; we are using this form to explore our ideas and passions. Even when you write to the same prompt (e.g., the college admission essay), I will encourage you to explore your unique view of the world.

Consider your audience:

Knowing whom *you are writing the piece for will help you decide* how *it should be written. An essay to a university admissions board will sound different than an essay in which you contemplate the effects of your parents' divorce. Knowing your audience as you draft is critical because it will shape so many of your decisions as you write.*

Consider your purpose:

Knowing why *you are writing this essay will also influence* how *you write it. We ask you to consider just what it is you want the reader to take away. Knowing your purpose and audience leads you to adopt a voice that serves both well. A letter written to inform the principal of the sexual harassment young women experience in the halls of the high school will be shaped differently than an essay that celebrates your love of the New York Mets. You might know your topic, but the act of writing itself can help you determine your purpose.*

Write your way into the paper:

Still don't know what to write? Great. Start writing. Sometimes we have to write a page or two before we discover what we want to say. The writing itself leads us to this discovery. *Don't be afraid of the blank page. Wrestling with the blank page weans you from dependence on the teacher. There will be more blank pages in your future.*

Choose an organization:

Through mentor texts, we will show you many ways you can structure essays. Do not be married to the first organizational structure you consider. We will teach you how to storyboard as a valuable tool when considering the many ways you might sequence the ideas in your essay. Play with rearranging your big ideas. An idea can resonate with power when placed at the end of the essay, like the last movement in a symphony. You want your essay to leave readers thinking, to pack a punch. Maybe this part near the end of your essay should now be the lead. Experiment. Ask a partner to read it. We expect you to decide on a structure that best delivers your message.

Consider the form:

Knowing your audience and purpose may help you to decide what form your writing will take. Is this writing more effective as a podcast? Will it become an extended poem? A multigenre blend of narrative and information to persuade an audience? This is a big decision. What's the most compelling vehicle to deliver your message?

Anticipate how readers will respond to your essay:

What do readers think as they read your essay? How will you address this response? Have you anticipated another point of view on your subject? Are there gaps in the story or argument? Are you able to use feedback in order to see your writing in a new way?

Ask for targeted response:

Writers solicit feedback. Analyze the weaknesses in your writing and revisit the questions that arise as you reread your draft. Ask for a focused response to your draft from your writing group, your teacher, or other readers. Select one or two areas in your draft that you would like your readers to comment on. Others can help you to understand where your writing is effective or not. Listen to them.

Play with word choice:

Reread your draft, word by word, sentence by sentence. Read it out loud. Does it sound the way you want the reader to hear it? Does your word choice match the tone you are seeking? Words have Velcro: there is a connotation attached to them. (Don't say skinny *when* slender *is more accurate.) Replace lifeless words.*

Play with sentences:

Does your syntax add power to what you are saying? Don't assume that the way you have structured the sentence in a first draft is the best way to write that sentence. Practice rearranging. Could a series of short sentences add power? How might you mix in complex sentences? Do your sentences build upon one another, creating a rhythm that adds momentum to your piece? Have you used any of the writerly moves we studied in passages?

Determine if you're ready to submit your essay:

> *We know your essay is not finished, because no essay is ever finished—but are you ready to let it go? Are you ready to let others read it as your best draft?*

Assessment and Grading

Formative Assessment

We have heard Barry Lane (2010) refer to formative assessment as "informative assessment," since it informs the teacher of the students' progress and helps to determine the next instructional steps. In Practice 8 we discussed how we use one-on-one conferences to assess what writers know and what they need, but we also design other formative assessments midunit. Following are some examples.

Question flooding: Students read drafts of their peers and flood their papers with questions. When we collect these drafts, we look at the patterns of questions readers asked and consider minilessons to address them. For example, is there confusion due to a lack of specific information in the opening of many students' drafts? The teacher could share the opening paragraphs from several mentor texts the next day in class. Students can highlight how key information is delivered in the openings of these essays.

Collaborative writing: We use collaborative writing when we give students complex assignments, like synthesizing multiple sources to support an idea. Working in partnerships, students practice weaving multiple sources of evidence into an argument. In an in-class assignment like this we supply the sources of evidence and the prompt, and we do not expect students to write an entire essay. We support students as they work together in class, and then we read their drafts to assess their effective use of synthesis. We share exceptional drafts in class the next day.

Prioritizing of needs: We collect a stack of student essays and read them only through a specific lens (e.g., do they move beyond summary?). We create a list of students who need additional help from this quick evaluation, and the next day in class we reteach the balance between summary and commentary to these students in a small group while others continue writing.

Big-picture list: As we read drafts, we keep a list of issues many writers are facing and give this list to the entire class. Students analyze their own drafts to determine if the items on the list apply to them (see Figure 1–12). You might create a T-chart to separate craft issues (e.g., lack of sensory details) from conventions issues (e.g., run-on sentences).

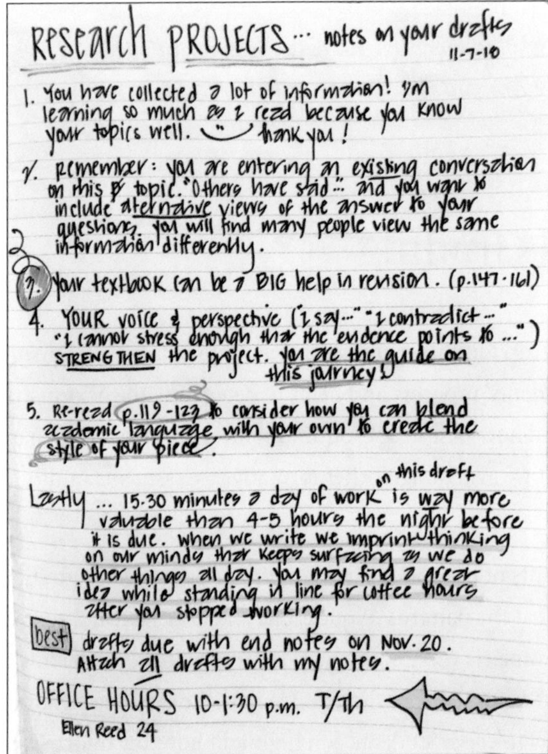

Research PROJECTS... notes on your drafts 11-7-10

1. You have collected a lot of information! I'm learning so much as I read because you know your topics well. :) thank you!
2. Remember: you are entering an existing conversation on this topic. "Others have said..." and you want to include alternative views of the answer to your questions. You will find many people view the same information differently.
3. Your textbook can be a BIG help in revision. (p.147-161)
4. YOUR voice & perspective ("I say..." "I contradict..." "I cannot stress enough that the evidence points to...") STRENGTHEN the project. You are the guide on this journey!
5. Re-read p.119-123 to consider how you can blend academic language with your own to create the style of your piece.

Lastly... 15-30 minutes a day of work on this draft is way more valuable than 4-5 hours the night before it is due. When we write we imprint thinking on our minds that keeps surfacing as we do other things all day. You may find a great idea while standing in line for coffee hours after you stopped working.

best drafts due with end notes on Nov. 20. Attach all drafts with my notes.

OFFICE HOURS 10-1:30 p.m. T/Th

Ellen Reed 24

Figure 1–12 Penny's Class Notes Given to All Students After Reading Drafts

None of these formative assessments is graded. They change our teaching, reminding us that we can never plan our entire course of study day by day before we begin a unit. We are teaching writers, not units. We need to be responsive to their unpredictable needs.

Summative Assessment and Grading

Grading is not only confusing but may actually cause harm. As one recent meta-analysis found, "Compared to those receiving comments, those students receiving grades (and no feedback) had poorer achievement and less optimal motivation" (Koenka et al. 2019). So we will be frank: we do not grade most of what our students write. Four things have made our students better writers—a volume of practice, choice, modeling, and feedback. Grading is not on this list.

Too much grading also places an enormous burden on teachers. If they must evaluate every essay for quality, it takes a great deal of time. Teachers get overwhelmed and avoid the stacks of papers covering their desks. We put it off. Students stop writing until the teacher can catch up. As volume decreases, students are denied necessary practice. The house of cards collapses.

So the best way to handle the paper load is to not create the paper load. Stop grading everything. Rely more on giving credit or no credit. For example, students write six essay drafts and select one to develop into a graded piece. They get credit for the six drafts, but only one is graded. The ungraded drafts remain part of the student's ongoing collection of writing. All writing—graded or not—remains in the portfolio.

Our schools—and our students and their parents—expect grades, so we grade some essays. We use criteria (created with students by studying mentor essays) to holistically score their essays. We share this criteria in the next section. Because we don't ever see a draft as final, we generally write two comments on each graded essay: we highlight at least one element we really like in the essay, and we provide one nudge in case the writer may want to go back and work on the essay some more. We do not grade with the intention of sorting students; we grade to encourage growth. No essay is ever finished—even if graded—and we remind students that their best work is yet to come. It will be showcased in their end-of-the-course portfolio (discussed later), which will largely determine their final grade in the class.

Individual Essay Grading

We determine criteria for excellence with our students as we study mentor texts together throughout the unit. Students should have a clear understanding of how excellence is defined. This does not, however, mean we create a rubric of this criteria. In *Writing Unbound*, Tom Newkirk discusses why he avoids rubrics:

> I refuse to have my reaction parceled out in traits or features. I will try to stay whole, to view writing as a human action that invites me to be attentive, curious, and generous—to be in a relationship—helpful, I hope, but not objective, because I am attending to a human gesture and not an object. (2021, 128)

We ask our students to write endnotes in order to reflect on what they have learned as they have developed their writing. They attach these to their best drafts. We read their endnotes before we evaluate their essays. Students briefly reflect on the following:

- Which mentor text had the biggest impact on your thinking and writing?
- Name a skill that you sharpened over the course of this unit.
- If you had more time to work on this, what would be your next move?

- Explain some choices you made while creating this draft.
- Is there something you want me to know about your process that is not evident in the best draft?

Self-reflection deepens students' thinking about their writing, and it provides us with invaluable information. We agree with John Warner, who says, "We seek to provide experiences designed around learning and growth, rather than giving assignments and testing for competencies. We will end the tyranny of grades and replace them with self-assessment and reflection" (2018, 141).

Part of this student reflection may include a student evaluation of their writing. It will be based on the criteria we have used throughout this unit to define excellence in essay writing.

Portfolio Grading

Summative assessments are sometimes graded and sometimes not. In a gradeless, portfolio classroom (as in Penny's college class), for example, students reflect on their ability to master the personal essay moves listed in the criteria for effective essays. Both teacher and student identify strengths and weaknesses of each product. Letter grades are not assigned to each best draft.

Both Penny and the student look at the completed work as a whole at the end of the course, analyzing the student's use of a writing process to improve drafts over time. The student submits a portfolio of all writing work to demonstrate proficiency across a wide range of skills in several rhetorical situations. The student writes an argument for the grade they have earned based on evidence in the portfolio. As part of this final argument, the student considers the decisions they had to make and the problems they solved:

1. Where did your ideas come from? Explain the ways you were led to your best writing.
2. How did reading impact your thinking and writing? Can you name specific craft moves you learned this semester and where you learned them?
3. What happened in between your drafts?
4. Tell about an important conversation you had about reading or writing this semester and how it impacted your work.
5. How are you a different writer than you were before you entered this course?

Excellence in Essay Writing

The criteria here, adapted from Catherine Lucas' work in the Puente Project—a University of California outreach program—remind us of specific moves we want to highlight during the teaching of this unit.

Scope

The writing exhibits a thoughtful treatment of a substantive topic. There is mature insight into one's or another person's life experiences, particular events, problems, situations, or conditions. The essay may exhibit elements of risk-taking. It illustrates connections between specific incidents and broader themes. The essay vividly relates a single significant event or sequence of events and strongly conveys the significance of the events or situation. The essay aims for insight.

Sequence

A strong controlling idea might focus on a character or person, a specific event, a sequence of related events, or a life passage, or the idea might focus on a community problem, legislation, or world issue. The essay may move in time and place, and the order of the essay is intentionally chosen to have an intended effect on the reader. The essay is organized with central points and events logically linked by well-focused reflection and analysis within and between paragraphs. There is a flow to the essay (no gaps), with appropriate transitions. The opening entices; the closing inspires thought.

Development

The topic or subject of your essay is developed with well-chosen, relevant, and sufficient details or evidence. The essay expresses insights fully developed by examples, explanation, research, extended metaphor, or analogy, and it anticipates and addresses the reader's questions or concerns. The controlling idea might be conveyed through specific actions, gestures, appearance, speech, or use of interior monologue. The idea might be conveyed through a synthesis of research, examples, reflection, and commentary.

Craft

The essay exhibits fluency with prose, precise language, and varied syntax. The writing has a rhythm that reinforces its message. The writer uses specific sensory details or complex analysis skillfully to establish and maintain an appropriate tone. There is a believable, consistent voice, which is tuned to explain, persuade, and address the reader directly.

Editing

The paper is edited for effect (e.g., a balance of long and short sentences, intentional fragments, paragraphing decisions). The paper exhibits attention to and control of conventions.

Again, we want to emphasize that we do not score each of these criteria separately. We see them as part of a tapestry of the entire essay, not as individual categories to be teased out. We do not assign points to each criteria. Isolating traits of writing and grading each minimizes the impact of the whole of the essay on a reader. In our notes to the student, we highlight elements in these categories that are successfully accomplished. We write "not yet" next to criteria that need more work. Penny gives feedback to her freshman composition students in a similar way, although the criteria change with the assignment (see Figures 1–13a–b).

Companion Arguments: conflict and solution letters

Substance: write with a passionate, informed, and credible **voice; synthesize your analysis of credible sources** you find while researching; use the **They Say/I Say templates** to honor those who have already studied your topic; use the depth of your research and your understanding of your subject to **persuade with power**

You have created a reasoned approach in both letters. I can tell you've practiced the habit of revision –

Organization: **hook your readers** with a compelling introduction which ignites interest in your subject; **summarize source material** and credit the sources of your information; **develop your claim** through to engage and inform readers; **conclude with new insights or challenges** to the reader to extend thinking

Your siblings & their differences were a powerful story to open with.

In your solution letter it would be smart to circle back to why you're telling this all to the Dept. of Labor.

Style: use **word choice** to create a believable, credible, consistent and **persuasive voice**; tune your voice to explain, persuade, and address the reader directly; **expertly craft words and sentences**; use repetition effectively in the style of Leonard Pitts, Jr. or Ibram X. Kendi

[illegible]

Your voice has a smart and engaging balance between serious and informal. Well done!

Correctness: **submit your letters to local or national media**; read your writing aloud to hear how it works and **fine tune your sentences** to match; balance long and short sentences; pay attention to **consistent verb tense**; use **paragraphs** to focus the reader on your main ideas; **cite sources** correctly in the text; polish your writing by **proofreading** line by line.

You took care to make these professional! :)

94 You've shown such growth this semester. Bravo!

Ghosts and Other Hauntings, 2020 Penny Kittle

Companion Arguments: conflict and solution letters — combined into one

Substance: write with a passionate, informed, and credible **voice; synthesize your analysis of credible sources** you find while researching; use the **They Say/I Say templates** to honor those who have already studied your topic; use the depth of your research and your understanding of your subject to **persuade with power**

Such a lot of convincing research to support this! Well done.

Who is the AJMC? Spell it out so people reading this know if they should trust your source.

Organization: **hook your readers** with a compelling introduction which ignites interest in your subject; **summarize source material** and credit the sources of your information; **develop your claim** through to engage and inform readers; **conclude with new insights or challenges** to the reader to extend thinking

Your personal story is a powerful addition, Zach. Well done. I'm so glad your younger brother has you to look up to!

Style: use **word choice** to create a believable, credible, consistent and **persuasive voice**; tune your voice to explain, persuade, and address the reader directly; **expertly craft words and sentences**; use repetition effectively in the style of Leonard Pitts, Jr. or Ibram X. Kendi

Your approach is earnest – I can tell you want people to understand. Well done.

Correctness: **submit your letters to local or national media**; read your writing aloud to hear how it works and **fine tune your sentences** to match; balance long and short sentences; pay attention to **consistent verb tense**; use **paragraphs** to focus the reader on your main ideas; **cite sources** correctly in the text; polish your writing by **proofreading** line by line.

To whom it may concern is less effective than directing your words directly to someone with the power to change things – like the Frost House here at PSU.

Needed to separate your big ideas into ¶s:
1. How many people affected
2. technology
3. the tragic story of your younger brother – I'm so sorry.
Yes! → 4. uncontrollable factors
5. Diet
closing … what to do. Sincerely, Zach, etc.

86 Do these ¶s make sense?

Ghosts and Other Hauntings, 2020 Penny Kittle

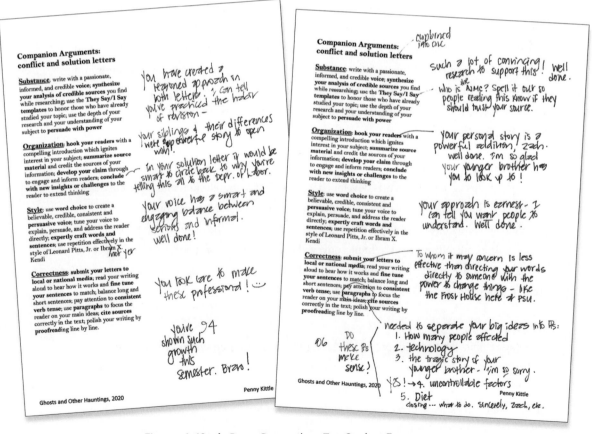

Figures 1–13a–b Penny Responds to Two Student Essays

Closing Thoughts

When we agreed to write an essay for *Educational Leadership*, we had to extend our thinking beyond the level of a tweet, an Instagram photo, or a text message. It's easy to share a thought in 180 characters or less; it's a lot harder to take an idea and develop thinking around it. Our article, "The Curse of 'Helicopter Teaching'" (Gallagher and Kittle 2020a), went through many iterations as the act of writing itself led us to thinking that surprised us. We were driven to do this work because we care deeply about the topic.

Mitzy found this drive when she wrote to both of her state's senators about the lack of mental health services available for students. As a daughter of undocumented parents, she recounted the years of xenophobia she had suffered, the threat of deportation that permeated her family, and the effects of poverty and racial injustice on her well-being in her letters. Mitzy believes these issues are particularly profound for the children of immigrants. When we read her letter essay, we felt her pain, her passion, her commitment.

Mitzy did not receive a response from the senators, but in naming the struggles she and others have faced, she felt empowered to start a student group at Plymouth State University called the Latinx Student Union (LSU+A). This organization brings students of Latin or Hispanic origin together with allies to study current issues, promote diversity, and show appreciation for the Latin and Hispanic community. All because of one essay.

Writing essays empowers students to make decisions, to show their thinking, to interrogate their sources, to have their say, and, as in Mitzy's case, to take action. If we boil this down, we want students to identify a big idea and to extend their thinking. We want students to discover the freedom and possibility of exploring the meaning of their lives through the art of essay writing. This is especially true for students who have been traditionally silenced and marginalized. Have we heard and honored their stories?

BOOK Clubs

The Best Teacher of Reading Is the Reading

> The desire to run the whole repertory of the classics down the throats of unresponsive students implies admission of defeat, the assumption that once out of our influence, they will turn no more to good literature. We need not fear the persistence of our present low cultural level, however, if we concentrate, not on force-feeding of the classics, but on the nourishing of a personal awareness of the joys of literature, and a capacity for critical judgment. We shall then send forth from our schools and colleges men and women eager to turn spontaneously to literature, as their own life creates the need, able to distinguish and to assimilate the good and great, wherever it manifests itself, in the literature of the past and of the present.
>
> **—Louise Rosenblatt, *Making Meaning with Texts***

We regularly read research on the teaching of reading. We recommend all teachers do. We also study our current students' habits and behaviors throughout the school year. We are committed to their development as lifelong readers and writers. If there weren't research to support the benefits of book clubs, we would deeply question why, since the evidence is clear in watching our students. But in fact, there is an abundance of research focused on the power of small communities of students reading and learning together (see Ivey and Johnston 2013; Cherry-Paul and Johansen 2019).

However, there is something we *can't* seem to find in research: how teaching a year of whole-class novels builds all students' engagement and the habit of lifelong reading. When large populations of adolescents refuse to read what is assigned to them, and also do not read for pleasure outside of school, our curriculum needs revision. We should start by including not only books that represent the lived experiences of our students but books that open new worlds to them (Bishop 1990). It is worth noting that Dr. Rudine Sims Bishop called for this revision more than thirty years ago. We want all students to experience the joy and discovery of learning from books, which means revising our curriculum.

A volume of reading is necessary practice to become strategic readers. When our students are in book clubs, they read more. They hold each other accountable, which spurs them on. Book clubs build a student's capacity for reading hundreds of pages a week. They are so essential that we build in opportunities for students to participate in them throughout the school year.

Beyond our classrooms, book clubs are an integral part of our personal reading lives. Kelly founded a book club with his colleagues in 1993 and has since read and discussed over two hundred books with fellow faculty and staff members. Penny runs a book club for hundreds of teachers every summer through her Book Love foundation. Book clubs motivate us to read. They deepen our understanding of not only the book but how others read and interpret the same text. Book clubs stretch our thinking, and they expose us to books and authors we may have otherwise missed.

We know that choice engages adolescents. When we ask students to choose books to study, they will often invite their friends to read with them. We watch students in groups of three to four form close-knit book clubs and dig deeper into their thinking in response to what they're reading. They talk more because they are *actually* reading and preparing for discussion, and they are more comfortable sharing their ideas when the spotlight of an entire class is not turned on them alone. A group is less intimidating; all group members begin to ask questions and listen to answers. This small-group experience deepens their understanding of the value of books and each other.

Our Beliefs About Book Clubs

Belief 1: We must build reading momentum *before* students enter book clubs

It would be a mistake to dive into our book club unit without first recognizing the scaffolding necessary to position students as productive book club members. This scaffolding begins with reestablishing an independent reading habit at the start of the school year after a summer (or more) of not reading. It is painful to admit, but most teenagers have stopped reading books altogether. As we've already noted, interest in books has fallen to an all-time low (Twenge, Martin, and Spitzberg 2018). Our student surveys confirm this year after year: they are not reading. We should not ignore what students are telling us.

It is imperative that we reignite an interest in (and a sustainment with) reading. When students choose what they read, they read more. Likewise, telling students who have stopped reading that they will begin the year by reading *Macbeth*—or any complex core text—is nonsensical. None of us would jump into class five rapids if we hadn't been in a kayak in months. But let's be honest, our kids are not even getting in the water. They are standing on the shore, watching us paddle. Our first challenge is to reengage all students in the regular act of reading. We focus our attention on building momentum and establishing individual reading identities—two critical factors that need to be in place *before* book clubs can soar.

Book clubs inspire readers to read more, and more matters. This belief may challenge your thinking about teaching reading. We ask you to look more closely at how reading for a teacher is different than reading for yourself. If we want to cultivate readers who will read with us *and without us*, we can start by examining the differences, as shown in Figure 2–1).

Reading for personal pleasure matters because it builds stamina for reading whole books. In doing so, students develop the confidence to handle difficult reading without teacher help—a skill needed in college and the workplace. Professors often ask students to read entire books independently. When Penny's daughter, Hannah, took Western Civilization as a freshman, she had to read a newly published work of nonfiction. Her assignment was to write an extended essay that analyzed the author's *position* on the subject of the book and how that position was influenced by the events described throughout the book. Not only was this book not summarized on SparkNotes, but the question was too broad to answer after a cursory reading. The professor did not dissect the book in class; to write the essay, students had no choice but to critically read hundreds of pages. We can't help but wonder: How many students would be prepared for this challenge based on their middle and high school ELA experiences?

In 2017 the official four-year graduation rate for US students attending public colleges and universities was 33.3 percent. The six-year rate was 57.6 percent. At private colleges and universities, the four-year graduation rate was 52.8 percent, while 65.4 percent earned a degree in six years (O'Shaughnessy 2021). Penny has found these statistics echoed in a disturbing pattern with her first-year students at a public university: they try to do school by not reading, and they begin to fail courses in the first semester. They are not used to failing—after all, their high school grades were good enough to get them into college. But when they start to fail, they become convinced that they do not belong in college, and too many of them drop out. (Twenty-five percent of Penny's students did in each of the last two semesters.) College students have discovered—painfully—that it is impossible to run a marathon if you trained by only running quarter miles.

Reading for the Teacher	Reading for Yourself
1. Reading is mostly about answering a teacher's questions by extracting information from a text. You read because you have to. The one who asks the questions is the one who will determine what kind of thinking will (and will not) occur.	1. Reading is a transaction between the reader and the text: you bring yourself to the reading and this changes what you notice in the text, what you connect to, what you question and explore, and what you remember about the book. Your thinking is not boxed in by anyone.
2. Compliance drives your engagement with the text.	2. Curiosity drives your engagement with the text.
3. You answer the teacher's questions to prove you've read. These questions halt your momentum because they require you to repeatedly stop and answer them. Answering someone else's questions gets in the way of asking your own.	3. You ask questions and explore your own thinking as you read. This leads you to consider when and where to stop instead of relying on someone else to make that determination. At other times you speed along because your engagement would be disrupted by stopping.
4. You lean on sources (outside of yourself) for understanding the content as soon as it becomes difficult. This is schoolwork, so efficiency is most valued.	4. You wrestle with the text. You become comfortable with ambiguity as your understanding unfolds. You may or may not seek sources outside of yourself, but first you wrestle to understand it.
5. You regularly practice performative scholarship. You haven't thought much about the book, but you can pretend you have. You are rewarded for your performance with good grades, but you know you were dependent on others to come to those understandings. You do not build confidence and independence as a reader.	5. As Ivey and Johnston found, "Once engaged, students learned that they were able to resist distraction and persist for extended periods, giving them a sense of self-regulation, which they then recognized as a personal competence. . . . A sense of agency and competence comes about when students realize that they can achieve a goal they value through strategic action" (2013, 14). You build confidence by working through confusion in complex texts.
6. When teachers choose a book, adolescents are often demotivated. The teacher becomes a salesperson trying to convince students that they should spend a month reading something selected for them.	6. When readers choose a book, there is initial buy-in. They are more likely to get started if they can select a book that personally connects. They are developing agency by not relying on the teacher to decide what is worth reading.

Figure 2–1 Reading for School Versus Reading for Yourself

Belief 2: Rigor is not in the book itself, but in the work students do to understand it

Some English teachers believe that when kids are all in the same text, and teachers direct that reading, it ensures that the experience is rigorous. For example, when students can't answer a question, a teacher will guide them back to the text and help build an understanding for them. If what matters most is the symbolism of the witches in the opening scene of *Macbeth*, then we can say that this approach works.

This is not what we mean by rigor. If students rehearse plot points and repeat platitudes gleaned from lecture or SparkNotes, they are not engaging in actual reading and thinking. In class discussion these students perform semblances of thinking but don't actually think very much about the book. Teachers who have lined their curriculum with hard books often use the texts as evidence that their classes are rigorous. But a complex book does not teach students how to read well; the work students do to make meaning of a text teaches them to read well. There is a mismatch between our ideals and the actual work many students are doing. Students often regularly see reading as one more task to complete to earn a grade for school, so they seek the easiest way to complete the work and move on. Yes, they may learn that Jay Gatsby pursues the American dream, but they do so without any intellectual lifting. (Alas, they've also missed the surprise of the elegant writing craft in that book.) Students have learned to game the system instead.

Teachers have told us they can't get students to even read the class novel, let alone evaluate the ideas there. We have experienced this struggle. But this lack of intellectual work with reading is why students like Jillian, whom we introduced in the first chapter, find themselves struggling after high school. In college, almost all reading is independent. Jillian could fake read in high school and still get good grades, but the fact that she did not develop reading stamina—and strategic reading practices—is harming her now. The task of reading entire books is beyond her frustration level.

Let's be clear here. We are not arguing that we should completely abandon whole-class novel studies. In *180 Days* (Gallagher and Kittle 2018) we showed how whole-class novels can be part of a balanced reading diet that includes independent reading and book club reading. Today we both believe the study of *Stamped*, for example, would be an excellent whole-class anchor for book clubs on racial equity. But first, we must get our students reading again.

We hear: "But my students won't read hard books on their own." We disagree. A study of engaged readers by Gay Ivey and Peter Johnston, published in *Reading Research Quarterly*, found that students read more and read *more challenging* texts on their own because "students' choices were based on personal relevance, regardless of difficulty" (2013, 18). We have seen many students persist with books that were far more challenging than we expected. Shane, a tenth grader, read *Moneyball*, which was far more difficult than anything he'd read before. He is fascinated by the influence of statistical analysis in Major League Baseball because he is a baseball player. We should never underestimate the power of students to persist in books that fascinate them.

Ivey and Johnston also studied the strategic reading practices of independent readers. They found that

> [students'] reported sense of agency in reading and persistence through challenging texts ironically resembles the performance and dispositions that seem to be the goal of common approaches to skill and strategy instruction. Strategic behavior for these students, though, appeared to be *less the result of strategy instruction than a response to their own need to make sense*. Their reading processes suggest that although it is possible to teach particular strategies, *instructional time might be better spent supporting engaged reading, a context in which students are more likely to actually become strategic*. (2013, 18–19, italics ours)

Ivey and Johnston are not suggesting we don't teach strategies, but rather they're asserting that unless students are engaged in making sense from the reading for themselves, they will not *use* those strategies. As Gay Ivey explained in a conversation with Penny, "uncertainty, coupled with caring, is a powerful motivator" (Kittle and Ivey 2019, 9).

Independent reading practice is the foundation for building critical thinking skills. As Seana Moran and Howard Gardner assert, "If a teacher does not provide real choices, if everything is mandatory and compulsory, there is no impetus to develop mental flexibility or cope with uncertainty" (2018, 33).

If we want to develop mental flexibility and teach students to cope with uncertainty in a text, it would be useful to consider the difference between guiding students through the reading of a novel and allowing students to read independently (as shown in Figure 2–2 on the next page).

Now we ask again, which practice is more rigorous?

We believe independent reading and book clubs lead our students to deeper thinking than whole-class novel study.

There. We said it.

Let us pause for a moment as you collect yourself.

Guiding Students in a Core Text	Allowing Students to Read Independently
1. Students *recall* the names and events in a text. Students are often directed to do this recall by answering a teacher's questions. Reading becomes an extraction exercise. Extracting information is not the same thing as the transaction between reader and text that noted educator Louise Rosenblatt ([1940] 2005) explored.	1. Students practice fix-it strategies in order to *understand* the characters and events as they read. They might see the name of a character and think, *Who is this again? Whom is this character connected to?* and then skim back through the text to answer their own question. Because answering the question is driven by curiosity instead of compliance, the act itself is a practice of the process of reading well without help.
2. Students can *explain* the big ideas in a text. Even if students haven't read *Gatsby*, they can say it is about the American dream and even quote events or "evidence" to support that claim because it is easy information to find online without reading.	2. A reader does more than *explain* the big ideas in the text. When the reader's mind follows the narrator of a novel, the immersion in experience takes them to intellectual places that are richer, deeper. Entering the experience results in students reckoning with their own moral dilemmas. This leads to a natural *analysis* of what is happening in the text and why. An engaged reader becomes the book and imagines being with the characters (Wilhelm 2007).
3. Passage study helps students to understand a particular passage, but it is often performed as a one-and-done act. For many students, the connection and transfer to the whole of the book is missing. The reader mimics the teacher or others who have analyzed the text.	3. The student who reads one self-selected Matt de la Peña novel is often motivated to read another, thus establishing a chain of reading. (It was common in our classes for students who had read one book they chose to ask for other books by that author; in contrast, it was incredibly rare for students whom we took through *1984* to ask to read another George Orwell book.) Building these reading chains encourages students to *synthesize* across an author's works, which is more sophisticated than *analyzing* one text alone. Reading several books by one author also pushes students to *evaluate* an author's contribution to a genre.
4. Readers often piece together their understanding of the book by reading SparkNotes, listening to the teacher and to classmates, and jumping around the chapters to answer the teacher's questions.	4. Readers are much more likely to read the entire book, thus developing their ability to hold on to their thinking over three hundred pages. The practice of holding onto thinking for hundreds of pages leads to a feeling of accomplishment. This is important in an age where too much out-of-school reading is click-and-go.

Figure 2–2 Reading with Guidance Versus Reading Independently

Although we have shared this approach with numerous teachers, we have encountered resistance. One curriculum director told us that her teachers do not see how independent reading is a meaningful part of instruction. When students are reading their individual books, her teachers told her, there is no teaching. They also feel that independent reading is not rigorous enough to justify sacrificing precious classroom time. Students would be better prepared, they argue, if instead they guided them through a challenging whole-class novel.

We understand where this is coming from. Like most teachers, we want the progression of skills and units over the course of the school year to be orderly. In addition, we love showing students how to unravel the complexity of the novel and its place in American culture.

But we must challenge the assumptions the resistance rests upon. Not only is it not rigorous to *pretend* to read a book, it is not even hard. And when the journey through a book is mapped out by somebody else, students become followers. Shouldn't students determine what the book means to them?

Belief 3: Students practice the habits of lifelong readers when they engage in book club conversations

Students are social—they crave time to connect with others and think together—but this simply does not happen enough in whole-class discussions, no matter what the text. There are two reasons: it is easy to hide in a class of thirty, and if students haven't read the book, they are not going to jump into a discussion where follow-up questions could reveal their deception.

In book clubs students choose the book, so they are more likely to *actually read*. When only four desks are huddled together, students are more likely to talk with peers. They not only engage with characters' emotions and motives but also ask questions about the moral dilemmas the characters face. Students turn inward from the reading, and the small-group setting makes it more likely they will discuss how these same dilemmas exist in their lives, as Gay Ivey and Peter Johnson found in their study of eighth-grade book clubs. Reading was no longer a "spectator experience," but one shared with peers. This made the act of reading one that built relationships within their book club, yes, but also within their classroom and school community" (2013, 17).

This engagement itself is satisfying to students, which is why book clubs that feature contemporary literature and nonfiction are an essential study. Ivey and Johnston continue, "Some students also admitted to having begun the year with a simmering anger because of their personal, economic, or family situation, but *reading books in which plausible characters, with whom they could relate*, have lives as hard or harder than theirs, gave them a different perspective on their own lives" (10, italics ours). This is exactly what we are looking for: purposeful, student-driven talk about books that moves beyond the book to life itself. These are the habits of lifelong readers.

Practices Most Important in Teaching Book Clubs

We have five essential practices for facilitating book clubs. They include choosing relevant books, connecting readers from different schools, balancing a volume of practice and close study, increasing student-directed talk, and giving students the power to make decisions.

Practice 1: We choose books that are relevant

In 2017 we shifted the theme of our book clubs to social justice. Why social justice? White supremacist marches occurred in Charlottesville, Virginia, and in other places. The president of the United States referred to Mexicans as drug addicts and rapists. An alarming number of videos surfaced depicting adolescents engaged in racist acts. The country argued about Colin Kaepernick and the take-a-knee movement. A debate about banning Confederate flags simmered again in Penny's high school. We didn't pick the theme of social justice; the theme picked us.

We realize social justice is too important a topic to be relegated to one unit in a school year. In order to practice being antiracist, we must examine *every* text we use in our classrooms: Whose voice is heard? Whose voice is missing? In our first attempt at designing book clubs around issues of injustice, we selected the twelve books listed in Figure 2–3.

From young adult fiction to Pulitzer Prize–winning nonfiction, these books represent a range of complexity in both length of text as well as depth of ideas. Students sampled each of these to decide which book they most wanted to read. We did not group our students; they grouped themselves by their selection of books. Sometimes, however, we stepped in to keep the groups at manageable sizes. When fifteen students selected *The Hate U Give*, for example, we subdivided those students into three different groups.

Fiction	Nonfiction
• *Refugee*, by Jason Reynolds and Brendan Kiely	• *Hillbilly Elegy*, by J. D. Vance
• *The Hate U Give*, by Angie Thomas	• *Just Mercy*, by Bryan Stevenson
• *All American Boys*, by Alan Gratz	• *There Are No Children Here*, by Alex Kotlowitz
• *The Sun Is Also a Star*, by Nicola Yoon	• *Evicted*, by Matthew Desmond
• *New Boy*, by Tracy Chevalier	• *The Short and Tragic Life of Robert Peace*, by Jeff Hobbs
• *American Street*, by Ibi Ziboi	• *Revolution*, by Deborah Wiles

Figure 2–3 Social Justice Book Club Choices

One important note: This list is malleable. For example, as some of our students read and discussed *Hillbilly Elegy*, we came to see the book as problematic. We read criticism online. We listened, and we now understand that there are better choices to capture Appalachian life. We apologize to anyone in the Appalachian community who may have been offended by this initial selection.

When the unit was over, we did what we always do: we asked ourselves what went well and what might be changed the next time we design a book club experience. We looked at the book selections, asking ourselves which titles were the strongest and which ones should be replaced. We surveyed our students, asking them which notebook provocations held the most relevance for them. And we considered the timing and sequence of the interaction between our classes. During this conversation we came up with a new way for our students to experience book clubs across the country: the study of writing craft through the work of one author. The author-study book club included the texts listed in Figure 2–4, by Matt de la Peña.

As the world evolves, so do our book club selections. In 2020, the murders of Ahmaud Arbery, George Floyd, Breonna Taylor, and others forced Americans to a racial reckoning. At our southern border, film crews showed young children in cages. Penny compiled a new round of books that would lead students to study how injustice and stereotypes haunt our lives in America. She asked students to choose two books from the following list, so that each student would read two books: one in the first four weeks of the year, followed immediately by a second book club with a different book. These books include issues of racial equity, immigration, and characters who struggle with mental illness:

The Nickel Boys, by Colson Whitehead

Dear Martin, by Nic Stone

Picture Books	Essay	Young Adult Novels	Short Story
Last Stop on Market Street *Carmela Full of Wishes* *Love*	"Why We Shouldn't Shield Children from Darkness," from *Time* magazine	*Ball Don't Lie* *I Will Save You* *Mexican WhiteBoy* *We Were Here* *The Living*	"Angels in the Snow"

Figure 2–4 Matt de la Peña Author Study

Sing, Unburied, Sing, by Jesmyn Ward

What Made Maddy Run, by Kate Fagan

We Were Here, by Matt de la Peña

We Are Not from Here, by Jenny Torres Sanchez

Long Way Down, by Jason Reynolds

How It Feels to Float, by Helena Fox

A Heart in a Body in the World, by Deb Caletti

We have also experimented with book clubs connected to a core text. In the first semester one year, Kelly made sure students experienced book clubs *before* getting to the study of a whole-class novel. The idea was a gradual increase in the perspectives they considered on one book: first their own independent reading, then in a small group, and then as a whole class.

But in the second semester he reversed the order of reading experiences by positioning thematic book clubs to *follow* core work study. In this case, Kelly picked books that extended the thinking found in the whole-class reading of *1984.* Why? Because he wanted his students to study big ideas across texts, across authors. We believe if students never independently practice synthesizing meaning across texts, they miss the joy and the intellectual rigor of questioning their understanding, expanding their thinking, and, most importantly, doing this work without a teacher's constant guidance. Following core work study with thematically related book clubs also gave our students an opportunity to see the relevance of the core work today. It enabled them to see what Kenneth Burke called the "imaginative rehearsals" found in classic literature are still being explored in contemporary literature and nonfiction (1968). It strengthened and widened their view, as they studied major themes through the eyes of more than one author.

While classics often remain static in English departments over decades, we select current books to extend the thinking of a whole-class novel. We interrogate what we teach and why. For example, Figure 2–5 lists book club selections Kelly chose to follow the twelfth-grade study of *All Quiet on the Western Front* in two different years.

Though you can teach *All Quiet on the Western Front* twenty-four years apart, the titles we select for the book clubs to follow the core text should be continually updated with contemporary authors and titles. This is not, however, an argument to teach *All Quiet on the Western Front.* It is a plea to update all curricula. You might begin by connecting contemporary literature to a core work.

All Quiet on the Western Front Book Club Selections in 1996	***All Quiet on the Western Front*** Book Club Selections in 2020
• *A Good Scent from a Strange Mountain*, by Robert Olen Butler	• *Fallen Angels*, by Walter Dean Myers
• *Johnny Got His Gun*, by Dalton Trumbo	• *All the Light We Cannot See*, by Anthony Doerr
• *Maus I* and *II*, by Art Speigelman	• *Matterhorn*, by Karl Marlantes
• *Shrapnel in the Heart*, by Laura Palmer	• *Redeployment*, by Phil Klay
• *The Things They Carried*, by Tim O'Brien	• *War Trash*, by Ha Jin
• *Voices from Vietnam*, by Barry Denenberg	• *The Cellist of Sarajevo*, by Steven Galloway
	• *The Good Soldiers*, by David Finkel
	• *The Nightingale*, by Kristin Hannah
	• *The Yellow Birds*, by Kevin Powers

Figure 2–5 Book Club Selections from 1996 and 2020

Core works must be updated as well. We think of Jesmyn Ward, for example, who along with William Faulkner, John Updike, William Gaddis, Saul Bellow, and Philip Roth, is one of only six authors to ever win the National Book Award more than once. Five white men and one Black woman. Why isn't Ward's *Salvage the Bones* or *Sing, Unburied, Sing* being taught in classrooms around the country as a core text? And wouldn't it be smart to pick book club selections to extend the thinking found in her complex novels? Or consider that Colson Whitehead is one of only four American novelists to win the Pulitzer Prize twice in fiction. He is the only Black man to have done so (the other three are white men). The selection of novels by Ward and Whitehead send a message. We must change the dominance of white voices in English curriculum and expand the literary canon to include a broad range of experiences written by people who have lived them. (See #OwnVoices for more ideas on book selection.)

Practice 2: We connect readers across schools

In *180 Days* (Gallagher and Kittle 2018), we talk about how our classes read *Romeo and Juliet* together. We put them in small book clubs to surround this text. We were struck by how having an audience outside the classroom elevated our students' interest. When students they did not know were waiting to respond to their thinking, both curiosity and engagement skyrocketed. Recognizing the power of connecting our students outside our schools, we added a third classroom to our social justice book clubs—college students from Miami University in Oxford, Ohio.

We both teach mostly first-generation-to-college students who lack confidence. We wanted to engage our seniors with current college students, so they could imagine themselves on campus in the fall. Dr. Kathy Bachelor's sophomore students at Miami were secondary English education majors, and we knew connecting them with our seniors would enrich everyone's learning.

We must emphasize this before we move on: *Nothing we did in this monthlong book study elevated our students' engagement more than connecting them to students outside the walls of our classrooms.* From three areas of the country (California, Ohio, and New Hampshire), our students encountered divergent thinking, life experiences outside of their own, and questions they hadn't realized they needed answered. One of Penny's students said she was hungry to hear from students who were not from her small town, and so she watched all of the posted discussions, even for books she had not read. We could not have provided this volume of speaking and listening practice, as well as the diversity of lived experiences that enhanced this unit, if we'd kept our book clubs in our classrooms.

Practice 3: We balance a volume of practice and close study

We plan for students to experience a balance of a high volume of reading, writing, and speaking along with frequent opportunities to slow down and participate in the close study of select passages.

A volume of reading

When we connect students from different schools, we want all students to complete the books in one month's time. We created a reading schedule to guide them. This schedule was a stretch for many, as students needed to read as much as 150 pages a week. Our students read at different rates, of course, which means that some of them worked hard to maintain the pace while others raced ahead and returned to their independent reading books while they waited for their book club peers to catch up. Some students downloaded the audiobook and listened to it on the way to and from school. An important reminder for both us and our students: the pace of reading hundreds of pages a week is common in college.

A volume of writing

Our book clubs included three ongoing requirements in writing: daily notebook writing in class, responses to focus questions, and the creation of student-generated two-page spreads to prepare for book club discussions.

We invite students to write next to poetry, infographics, editorials, and photographs as regular practice all year. During book clubs, we focus these invitations and provocations on the theme of the book club, which for the following examples was social justice. These were some of our choices:

Poems

"Take a Knee," by Kwame Alexander

"What the Dead Know by Heart," by Donte Collins

"Rigged Game," by Dylan Garity

"Allowables," by Nikki Giovanni

"Gate A4," by Naomi Shihab Nye

"Lay Her to Rest," by Josina Guess

"Manna," by Micah Bournes

Infographics

"Study: All-White Jury Pools Convict Black Defendants 16 Percent More Often than Whites," by Steve Hartso, *Duke Today* (we used only the infographic in this article)

"The Growth of Incarceration in the United States," from the National Academies of Science, Engineering and Medicine

"In 83 Million Eviction Records, a Sweeping and Intimate New Look at Housing in America," by Emily Badger and Quoctrung Bui, *The New York Times*

"State of the Dream 2016: #BlackLivesMatter and the Economy," posted by Mike Leyba on the website of United for Fair Economy (a national, nonpartisan, nonprofit Boston-based movement support organization that highlights the detriments of uneven wealth distribution)

"Mapping Prejudice," by the University of Minnesota (on racially restrictive deeds in real estate)

Digital commentary

"The Black Bruins," by UCLA athletes

"What Is Privilege?" from BuzzFeed

"Being 12: What Are You?" from WNYC

"We Need to Talk About Injustice," by Bryan Stevenson, TED.com

"America's Native Prisoners of War," by Aaron Huey, TED.com

"A Tale of Two Americas: And the Mini-Mart Where They Collided," by Anand Giridharadas, TED.com

Articles

"Please Rise for Our National Anthem—if You're Not Too Busy," by John Branch, *The New York Times*

"The Cancellation of Colin Kaepernick," by Ta-Nehisi Coates, *The New York Times*

"Black Men Sentenced to More Time for Committing the Exact Same Crime as a White Person, Study Finds," by Christopher Ingraham, *The Washington Post*

"The Private Prison Industry, Explained," by *The Week*

"Georgia Man's Death Raises Echoes of US Racial Terror Legacy," by Aaron Mortenson and Ross Bynum, *Associated Press News*

Each day, we shared one text and asked our students to write in response to it. We did not give them questions to spur this writing. Instead, we asked them to select an idea, a word, a phrase—any hot spot pulled from the text that helped them to deepen their understanding of the idea of social justice. As our students wrote, we wrote alongside them. After a few minutes of writing, we stopped and practiced a few minutes of daily rereading and revision. We told our students to read what they had written and make it better writing. We modeled this daily tinkering with our own crappy first-draft quickwrites in front of them because we wanted our students to understand that rereading and rewriting are habits. The more we practice, the better we write. As writer Lydia Davis said, "constant revision, whether or not you're going to 'do' anything with what you've written, also teaches you to write better in the first place, when you first write something down" (2019).

We didn't always pick the texts that we presented to students. About halfway through the unit, some of our students began to bring in relevant poems, infographics, and photographs that interested them. We created a digital page where we posted all student-selected texts, and on occasion, we directed our students to select which one to respond to. We also varied the length of time for initial quickwriting from four to ten minutes.

An author-study book club

We chose the works of Matt de la Peña to study in 2019, not only because he is an author of color, but because his books had already proved popular with many of our students. Matt has written across genres, from children's picture books, to short stories, to essays, to YA novels. For this book club, we asked our students to focus on how the author used writing craft moves across genres. We began the unit by sharing with our students the finish-line questions focused on craft. Although they continued to read in cross-country groups, our assessments were different, as shown in Figure 2–6.

Kelly's Finish-Line Questions (*High School*)	**Penny's Finish-Line Questions** (*College*)
Read Like a Writer: Analysis of Matt de la Peña's Craft Moves Matt writes haunted characters. What are they haunted by? How does Matt use elements of writing craft (sensory detail, repetition, etc.) to help you understand what these characters are struggling with? How does the author reveal this haunting (e.g., themes, craft, setting, behaviors)? In an essay you will analyze the moves and techniques employed by the author that bring his characters to life. You should share (1) specific moves—with cited page numbers—that you find effective along with (2) explanations as to why you believe these moves are important.	*Option 1: Claims you might make about Matt de la Peña's writing based on your observations, curiosity, and wonder:* • The character is believable, haunted even. Here's how . . . (Choose one character and focus, or pick two and contrast them.) • The description creates an image for readers. • The dialogue reveals character. (How? Where?) • The complex movement in time showed me . . . • Matt reveals racism, loneliness, homelessness. (How? Where?) *Option 2: How can you show an understanding of Matt de la Peña's craft?* • Write an analytical essay that supports one of the claims above (or your own). • Write a fictional story that imitates his writing craft moves and add footnotes that describe why each move is an important one in your story. • Write a short story in verse that imitates his craft moves (with footnotes). • Write a graphic novel that imitates his craft moves (with footnotes). • Create a podcast interview between characters and Matt or a reader and Matt.

Figure 2–6 Assessments for de la Peña Writing Craft Study

The study of picture books: We studied two of de la Peña's picture books, *Last Stop on Market Street* and *Carmela Full of Wishes.* Kelly asked his students to chart the structure of a story (exposition, rising action, climax, resolution). He then asked them to identify big ideas and to consider how these ideas were revealed and illuminated through both the author's writing and the illustrator's art. In Penny's class, students created found poems using the text of *Carmela Full of Wishes* to practice transforming one text into another.

Our students studied *Love* to look at how a big idea is developed through examples in words and in pictures. We had them do a close reading of one of the illustrations, by Loren Long (see Figure 2–7).

Our students inferred that the parents' argument was intense from some of the visual clues in the text: an empty cocktail glass, an overturned chair. We knew that de la Peña and Long had to fight their publisher to keep this illustration in the book, as there was a concern that it might be too heavy for young children. This raised an interesting question for our students to consider: Should young children be shielded from works that are emotionally complex? We studied de la Peña's essay for *Time* magazine titled "Why We Shouldn't Shield Children from Darkness." Not only did this generate interesting writing and discussion, but it also led students to analyze de la Peña's writing craft across genres. Students noticed some of the same moves in picture books and in his essay, but they also discovered moves in the essay that they had not seen in the picture book. We had our students chart these similarities and differences.

Figure 2–7 Loren Long Illustration from *Love*

The study of YA novels: We set up the reading of de la Peña's novels with weekly focus questions:

> Week 1: What do we know about these characters? What is said? What is implied?
>
> Week 2: We are all haunted (tormented, anguished, troubled, plagued, bedeviled, beleaguered, oppressed, obsessed, tortured, preoccupied, worried, disturbed) by events we've lived through or imagined. How are these characters haunted? And by what? How does the author reveal these hauntings?
>
> Week 3: What trouble is brewing? What does this trouble tell you about big ideas that are emerging?
>
> Week 4: What craft moves are you noticing? Can you add to the moves you noticed in Matt de la Peña's children's books and essay? What do you notice about the structure of the novel? What decisions were made in the construction of the story?

We created a one-month calendar that included weekly meetings. We brought in poems and de la Peña passages to generate quickwriting. We connected our students across classrooms via Flipgrid. We asked them to prepare for discussion by creating two-page spreads (see Practice 4) of their thinking as they read. In addition, we asked them to dedicate two pages in their notebooks to capture interesting, intriguing, and provocative language. We wanted students to consciously celebrate words and passages, as they had done in social justice book clubs.

The study of a short story: After students finished the novels, we concluded our unit by studying de la Peña's short story "Angels in the Snow." Much like we had done in the picture books, the essay, and the novels, we had students pay close attention to the writing craft moves made by the author. We revisited and compared these moves across genres as a way to prepare them for the finish-line questions.

We used this short story to sharpen our students' close study practice. We asked, "Can you find the significance of a character in a small detail?" Small details—what a character is wearing; the description of the setting; something a character says or thinks—often reveal big things. Students searched for a small detail that spoke loudly about a character. We modeled it with the example in Figure 2–8. We invited students to discuss their examples in book clubs.

Online book clubs

Penny's courses were moved online in the fall of 2020 because of the COVID-19 pandemic. She organized regular book club meetings for the first eight weeks of the semester. As with all things

Small Detail	Why Would the Character Do This?	Why Did the Author Make This Decision?
Shy lies: "Anyway," she said. "I have a little situation upstairs. When I try and turn on the water in the shower, nothing comes out. Like, not even a drizzle. Do you know about stuff like that?" "A little bit." *Lies!* "Need me to take a look?" "Would you?" "Lemme grab the keys."	Shy lies because he is immediately attracted to Haley and he is trying to find a way to extend his time with her.	The author is trying to show the reader that Shy felt an instant spark when he first met Haley. This immediately teases the reader into knowing that this story may be about romance. It puts us in Shy's corner—makes us root for him. Every reader has been in the same situation in our own lives. This builds empathy for Shy.

Figure 2–8 Analyzing a Small Detail

in 2020, what was once easy was now more difficult, and in this case, igniting conversations *between* students was complicated. In her classroom, desks are grouped together, and students' talk about books often starts before class does. No one waits for Penny to lead them. This results from an important teacher move: when we step back, we disappear from sight. Students forget we are nearby, allowing us to watch the flow of conversation and even eavesdrop, without students feeling their responses are being studied and judged.

Online, as Penny's face hovered in one of the boxes on the computer screen at the first book club meeting, conversation halted. *The teacher is here: don't make any sudden moves.* Penny knew she needed more than two-page spreads and open-ended questions to break the silence, which was now even more awkward online.

In class, students held up notebooks to share the passages and ideas they had been collecting with others during book club meetings. Online, no one did.

A combination of study, quickwriting, and sharing opened up these conversations. Penny began one meeting by playing two minutes of Chimamanda Ngozi Adiche's TED talk "The Danger of the Single Story" (2009). Adiche highlights the importance of power and how it determines whose story is told and how. Penny turned this to her students: "Think about the book you are currently reading: Who has power? Who doesn't?" She asked students to write for four to five minutes in their notebooks before beginning to talk. Writing together—even online—creates community. Students know they are not judged on this rough-draft thinking, so they are freer to find what they mean and want to say. Conversations burst forth and Penny could retreat to being an observer, instead of prompting the discussion.

She added Ibram X. Kendi's essay "Who Gets to Be Afraid in America?" (2020) to quick-writing the next week. Students wrote next to Kendi's ideas, and when they came to book clubs, she asked them to revisit their original thinking through the lens of the book they were reading. Those reading books about mental illness immediately made the connection to the stigma attached to depression and how this increases fear and uneasiness in those who are suffering.

The practice of writing next to engaging texts, photographs, and works of art is more difficult to achieve in online book clubs. Some students attended the virtual book club from common areas on campus and felt awkward writing from a public place. It is hard to focus when writing from the dining hall. Penny missed the silence of the classroom where all wrote in community. However, writing before talking focused and intensified book club discussions. Notebook writing can lead students away from the text. Subsequent discussion weaves the happenings in our current world with an author's invented world. It increases their understanding of both.

We want our students to experience book clubs more than once in a school year, so we plan more than one round of book clubs. Because each unit is a month long, our students spend a third of their reading year in book clubs. Providing three book club experiences allows students the opportunity to deepen their strategic reading skills through close study. It is a window into what we hope for their future: vibrant book club meetings that stretch them the way our book clubs stretch us. Book clubs strengthen reading muscles and build communities. In a word, they are *essential* in a balanced reading diet.

Practice 4: We increase student-generated talk

> Face-to-face conversation is the most human—and humanizing—thing we do. Fully present to one another, we learn to listen. It's where we develop the capacity for empathy. It's where we experience the joy of being heard, of being understood.
>
> —**Sherry Turkle,** *Reclaiming Conversation*

Establishing meaningful peer talk is a critical component to sharpening critical thinking skills. To do this, we have to move our students away from questions that test only their extraction skills. Following are the strategies we used to increase student talk in book clubs.

Open-ended discussion questions

In addition to the daily notebook writing, we asked students to respond to weekly focus questions on Google Docs that were shared across our two schools:

> Week 1: What's worth talking about? Is there a passage that struck you as important in developing a character or a person or an idea in the book thus far?
>
> Week 2: Name and discuss a big idea that is emerging.
>
> Week 3: Name and discuss the systems or institutions that contribute to equity or inequity.
>
> Week 4: How has this experience of reading and listening to others changed your thinking?

These questions were intentionally open-ended to spur fresh thinking.

Student-generated two-page spreads

Even though our book club discussion questions were open-ended, they were still provided by the teacher. We wanted our students to generate their own thinking before coming to book club meetings, so we asked them to prepare for discussion by creating two-page spreads in their notebooks. Our directions were not more sophisticated than that; we simply asked them to bring evidence that they had been thinking about their reading. Some students did not like this. They knew it was easier to simply answer the teacher's questions. What should they put on a blank page? We anticipated this resistance. We shared notebook observations we had made on one of the books. We encouraged students to collect what they found important in the text, to sketch if they chose to—to organize their thinking however it made sense to them.

We used examples from their peers. When students turned in the first round of spreads, we quickly combed through them, searching for varied examples. We flagged these and brought them back to class. We said, "Look at what Taylor did here; look at what Kalli did there." (See Figures 2–9a–f for some examples. These are also available as Online Resources 2–1 through 2–6.)

The student in Figure 2–9a made bulleted lists of what she considered important information from Chapters 1 through 4 of her book. Notice the categories: court case, racial profiling, Walter's time in court, and Herbert Richardson. We showed this under the document camera to remind students that organizing notes into categories is a smart strategy to make sense of a lot of information.

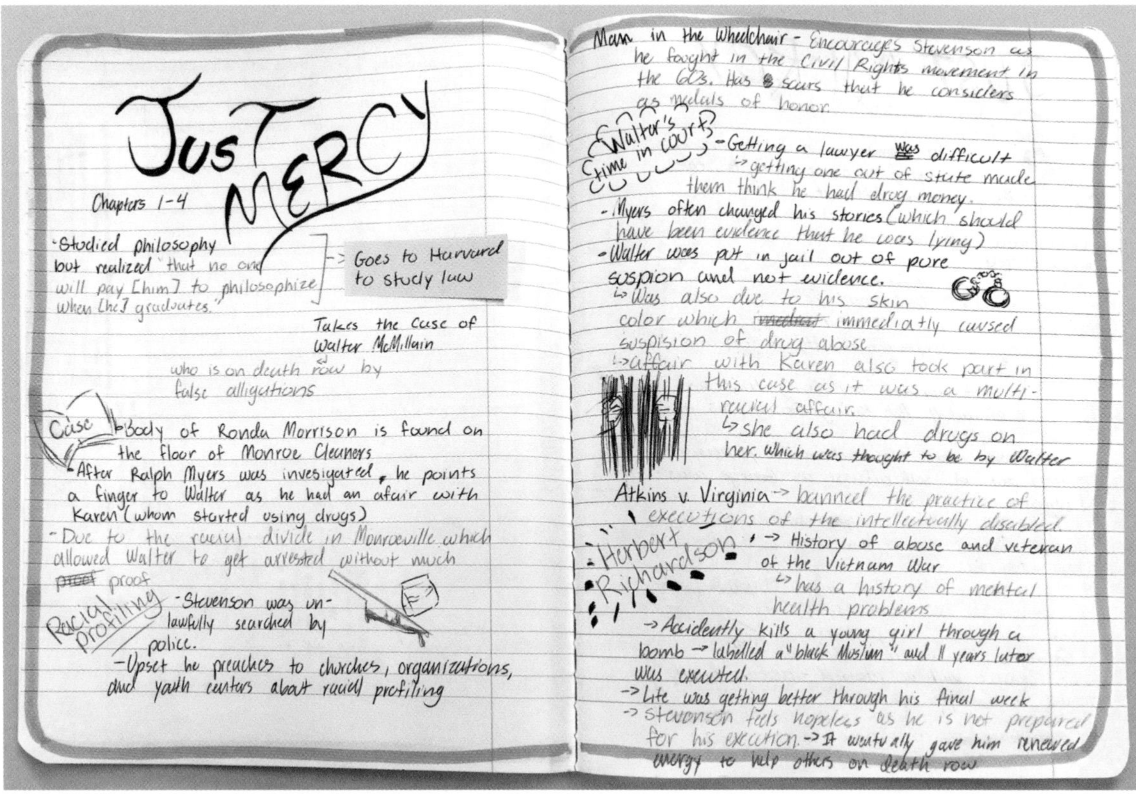

Figure 2–9a Two-Page Spread with Lists

The students whose work is shown in Figures 2–9b and 2–9c kept sticky notes in their books as they read and then added them to their notebooks before class. Notice how one of them used colors to categorize the kinds of notes she was taking on *I Will Save You* (Figure 2–9c).

Another student wrote two pages of notes and thoughts on the reading to prepare for the book club discussion and then highlighted points she felt were most important to share (Figure 2–9d).

Yet another student put the open-ended questions we posed at the top of the left side (Figure 2–9e). The student listed elements of writing craft as well as quotes from the text and thoughts. This is a different organizational system than the sticky notes examples, so we shared it with students as well in order to show that how they kept notes was as individual as they are.

Because many students were not used to generating their thinking without prompting from the teacher, some of them started slowly. But as the year progressed and students had numerous opportunities to share, their spreads markedly improved. Many found the freedom refreshing. As teachers, we celebrated their divergent thinking, and it made for richer discussions.

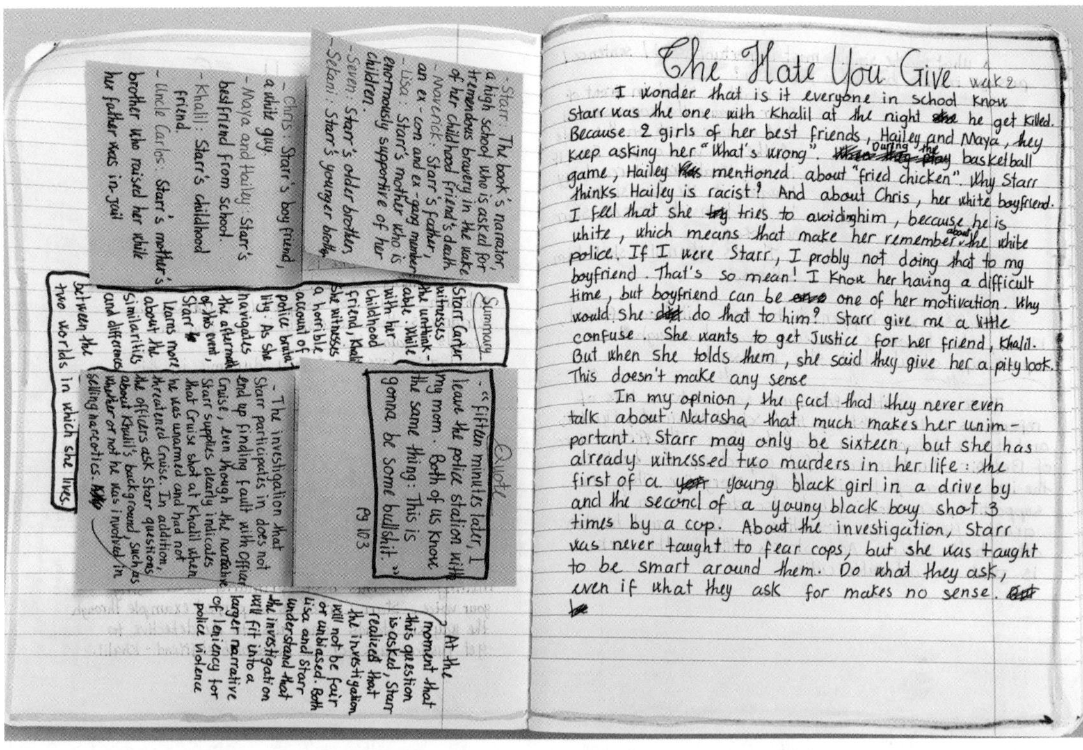

Figure 2–9b Two-Page Spread with Sticky Notes Transferred from the Book

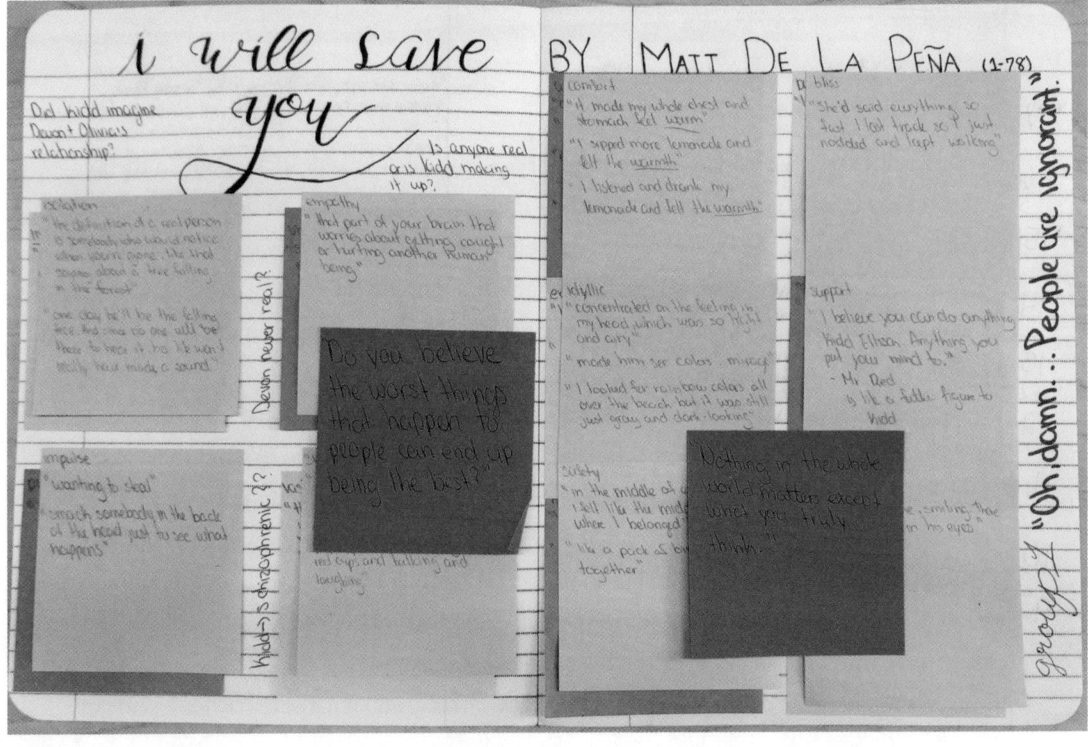

Figure 2–9c Two-Page Spread Organized with Different-Colored Sticky Notes

as I read so it ... make a ton of sense

9-04-19 I will Save You: Matt De La Peña

Matt writes Kidd to be this unforgiving murderer who killed Devon, his best friend. At the same time though, Kidd thinks about how he could've just separated soul mates. De La Peña writes Kidd (so far) to almost have two different personalities. One that ~~has~~ shows no mercy and one that thinks about a love story that he may have ruined.

I'm not certain about this, but it seems like he switches between past and present in the book. Or maybe different points of view. It switches from Olivia's letters / point of view to Kidd's.

Kidd, who killed his best friend has an obsession with Philosophy of Life books which seems ~~to~~ to conflict with him murdering someone.

While Kidd is having dreams about Olivia De La Peña sort of makes them seem like real life, but puts ~~[scribbled out]~~ Olivia's dialogue in italics.

In the beginning, there was a line that said "I'm hovering by the ceiling now. Next to my mom, we're both watching me lay here unable to move, chest going up and down and up and down, too many times a second."

I haven't been able to get that out of my head. For 20-30 pages I kept thinking about it, so I found it again. I have a couple of thoughts about it. The first thought is that he died and the rest of the book is him, but his ghost. The second thing is that maybe he was having an out of body experience and that was a fucking awesome way to show not tell.

Pg. 72- Devon pulls up and starts interrogating him about running away. He also starts sort of belittle Mr. Red to Kidd.

Okay. I think what they did is put a middle/end scene in the beginning (where Devon dies) and after that it's flashbacks and the full story leading up to Kidd pushing Devon off the bridge or whatever it was.

Pg. 75 "Trust me, girls love a challenge because they've been handed everything their entire lives." Devon is talking about him and Kidd I think because they're both "troubled" kids.

As Devon comes into the picture again, Kidd's old habits (sleep walking and shit) starts to come back. He knows Devon is bad for him like the little devil on your shoulder or the anxiety that keeps you up at night.

"People's faces tell more about what they're thinking than their words." ... I feel attacked by this because I relate soooo hard.

I don't think this is happening, but the way De La Peña writes Devon, he could honestly be Kidd's insecurities. Or he could be a voice in his head and Kidd could have schizophrenia. That would be a cool ass way to write this book! And when Devon dies, it could be Kidd killing ~~[crossed out]~~ the voice in his head, but he would also have to kill himself to do that! You can't kill the voices in your head without killing yourself! ... That was a good book idea!!

Figure 2–9d Two-Page Spread with Highlighted Points

I will save you - pg. 78-155

→ Week 2 - Guiding Qs ←
→ what big ideas are emerging?
→ What trouble is brewing in the plot?
What author's craft moves are you noticing?

Character	Qs. Character Development.
Kidd	- struggles with lots of issues - hard time feeling/process things - what other struggles? - Poverty
Olivia	- Why does she wear the ski-cap? - Poetic - oblivious to her affect on Kidd - What else about her?
Devon	- Why the Death Drive? - What is up with Devon? Life? Family? Up bringing? - poverty/low income/steals clothes - Care free attitude - Trouble Maker - reminds me of the joker

- Author's craft: * Flash Back: switches a lot from past from present *
- KIDD'S PHILOSOPHY of LIFE BOOK
 - Philosophy #3: About how a bad thing can turn good.
 → Pg. 88-90
 - talks about Mother in Hospital
 - Realized something good from bad

I Will Save You - Pg. 78-155

one word description: good, scary, bad, messy, influence, depression, blinded, differences, lust, kindness, trouble, love, manipulation, Will, save you

connections (IRL-Book-Any): Devon - Joker; Death Drive; no care; Personality, Dislike him; San Diego zoo; been there before!

Quotes:
- Mr. Red: "people should work to live, not live to work." - p.140
- Kidd "When he (Devon) escaped his group home at the start of summer, to find a really good friend me, the world became less safe" - p.142
- Devon: "We already know how meaningless we are. The world has already shown us. You could learn a lot from poor kids like me and him." pg. 138
- * Kidd: "When bad things happen to people they can have a moment of clarity where they realize what they have to do." - p.108

Thoughts:
- Devon is really driven by adrenaline
- Does Olivia like Kidd? Would they end up together?
- No, sees him more as a really good friend
- San Diego zoo trip with Red improved their relationship
- Fixing Cliff Fence foreshadows event from the beginning of the book
- Devon = real?

Figure 2–9e Two-Page Spread with Guiding Questions at Top

Two-page spreads can also be used in other content-area classrooms. A colleague of Kelly's, Susan Fried, had her students generate two-page spreads demonstrating their thinking in her anatomy classes (see Figure 2–9f for a spread created by her student Molly after reading a chapter on the structure of human tissue).

Talk about charts, tables, and graphs

While students were participating in their social justice book clubs, we overlaid a mini-unit on how to critically read charts. We began this practice by giving our students some charts to analyze, and for each chart we had them consider two questions: (1) What does the chart say? and (2) What does the chart not say?

Once they had practiced their summary and inference skills, we asked them to find charts that would deepen a reader's understanding of the books they were studying. For example, Katrina was reading Alex Kotlowitz's *There Are No Children Here*, which delves into the effects of poverty and violence in Chicago. Katrina researched and found a chart titled "Factors Influencing Local Gang Violence," which connected her thinking from the book to her world (see Figure 2–10). We asked each student to find two charts to augment the book they were reading

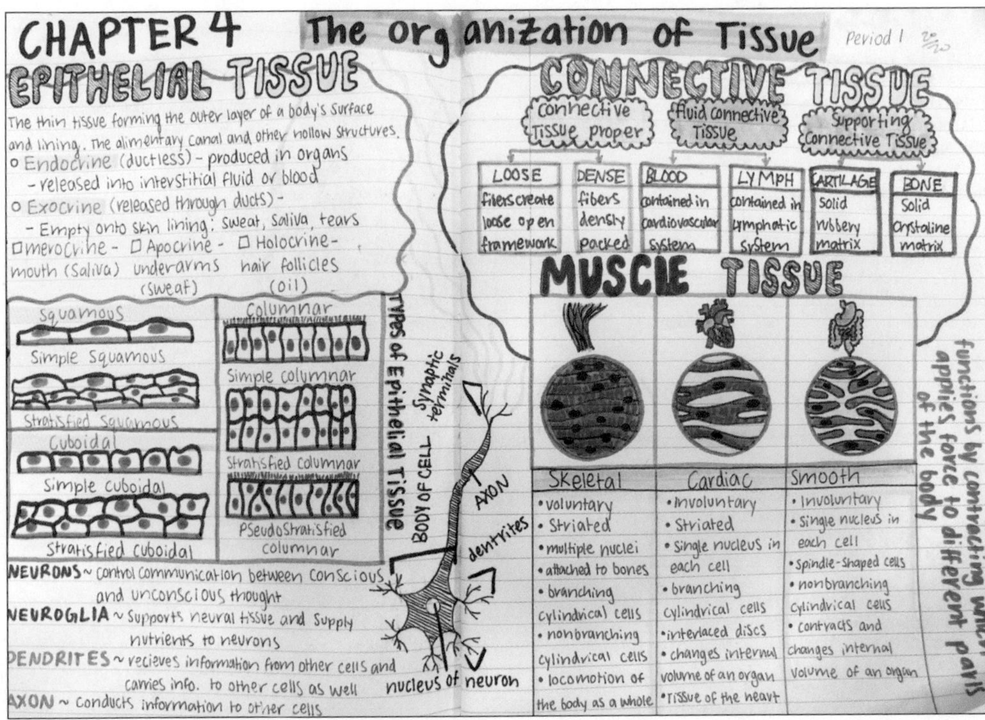

Figure 2–9f Two-Page Spread on Human Tissue

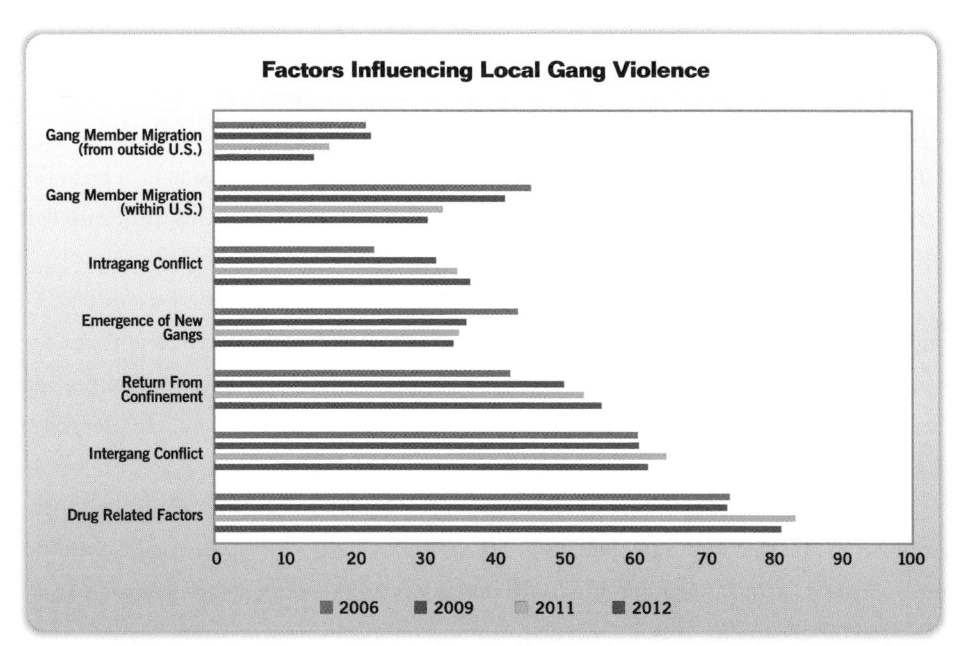

What does the chart say?	What does the chart not say?
• New gangs have slowly stopped forming • Gangs keep returning home from jail • Issues within the gangs remain very steady throughout the years • Usually between two or more gangs	• Where are these gangs mostly located? • Where did they originate? • Who was in charge of each gang? • What kind of conflict happens within each gang? • Where are gangs coming from if they are not from the US?

I would place this chart at the end of page 430, right before the beginning of chapter 26. King, who was the king of the King Lord Gang, had just set a fire in Maverick's store while all the kids were inside. He did it with the help of some boys from his gang but ended up getting caught. Everyone says that they saw him do it, even though they did not. They were tired of the gang violence in their community so they figured, if he went to jail for arson, he would not be able to return for a while.

The chart discusses what influences gang violence throughout cities. In this case it is because of intragang conflict, due to the fact that Maverick used to be in the gang, so since he used to be affiliated with them in the past, it affected his present life.

Figure 2–10 Katrina's Connections Between a Chart and Her Reading

and then consider a third question: On which page, specifically, would you place these charts in the book to deepen the readers' understanding? Choosing the place where each chart fits best is an act of literary analysis. This analysis, done by each member, results in vibrant book club discussions. Each student finds different charts, tables, or graphs. They share their thinking and their decisions behind the placement of those informational texts to talk about a reader's understanding of the big ideas in their books. We asked our students to do this work with fiction as well as nonfiction.

This work can also be done to develop critical literacy skills while reading a core text. For example, in reading the novel *1984*, one student selected a chart that displayed New York City's placement of surveillance cameras throughout the five boroughs. He could see the connection to the scene where Winston and Julia are caught by a hidden surveillance camera. This deepened his understanding of the dangers of modern-day governmental intrusion.

Students learn from repetition. If you implement this practice with a core text and then ask students to find charts for their book club books, they will develop greater facility with the reading of charts, tables, and graphs. Repeated practice matters if students are going to use this skill beyond the classroom. This is particularly important in a world where information is often condensed into graphic representations. More now than ever, charts, tables, and graphs are used to help us draw generalizations from data to explain events. We want our students to be critical readers of these texts.

Talk about key sentences and passages

We refer to the *study* of writing throughout our work. As practiced readers, we all learn to write by reading, sometimes without realizing it. However, the more clearly we make this connection for our students, the more likely they will benefit from it.

This is a practice that originated in Penny's classroom as part of independent reading, but we have both used it as an invitation to deepen thinking and discussion during book clubs. The directions are open-ended. We say to students, "As we read, we will be collecting sentences and passages from our books. When you come upon a sentence or a passage that you feel is important or well said, or simply beautiful, you add it to a two-page spread in your notebook." Some students imitate the cover art or sketch a symbol that matters in the book, as Sydney did in Figure 2–11a. She included the page number where she found each quote from the book, which helped her share the context of the passage when discussing it with her book club.

In Figure 2–11b, you can see that Christian had a combination of sticky notes with quotes he collected while away from his notebook and quotes he copied directly into his notebook while reading in class. He did not include art. This was his choice. There are no points assigned to this

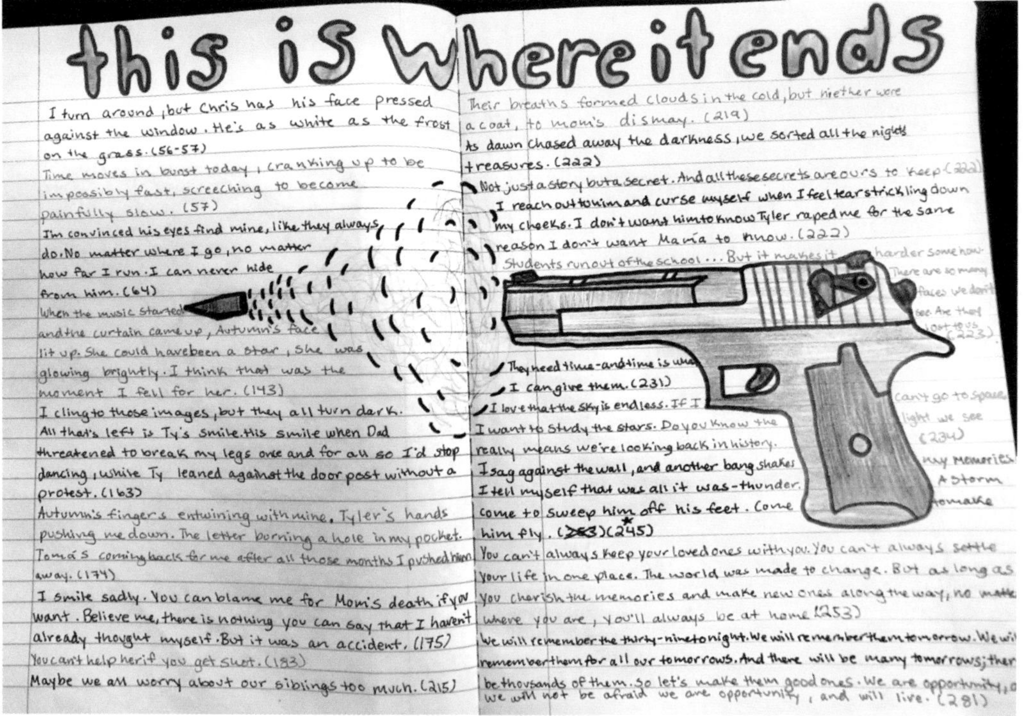

Figure 2–11a Sydney's Collection of Important Passages

task, no rubric. This is about paying attention to the writing craft authors use to make meaning. The collecting, and the way it deepens our thinking to pay attention to language, is the goal. Christian told Penny he understood the book much better as a result of the assignment to collect language, because each time he slowed down to record a passage, he thought about what was happening in the book as he copied it. You can find a collection of these student spreads under "Book Love workshop handouts" on https://pennykittle.net.

When students shared these collections in their book club discussions, they were drawn back to the text again and again. This close study of the writing craft led to rich thinking about the big ideas in the books. In Figure 2–11c you can see students engaged with this work.

Other close study practices we have used to generate talk

In the midst of all this volume of reading, writing, and speaking, we provided students with opportunities for close study. Close study is often directed by a teacher, so we want to be careful that we balance teacher-generated talk with student-generated talk, and if we have to pick which one gets more attention, we want our students' thinking to drive discussion. After they'd written

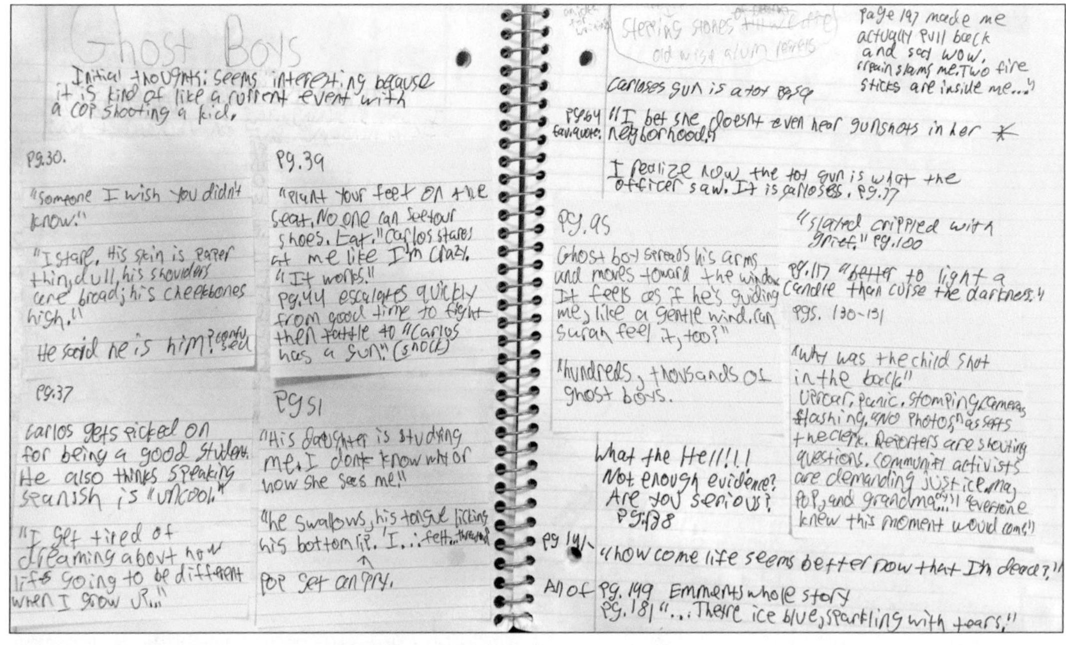

Ghost Boys

Initial thoughts: Seems interesting because it is kind of like a current event with a cop shooting a kid.

Pg. 30.

"Someone I wish you didn't know."

"I stare. His skin is paper thin, dull, his shoulders are broad; his cheekbones high."

He said he is him? confused

Pg. 37

Carlos gets picked on for being a good student. He also thinks speaking spanish is "uncool."

"I get tired of dreaming about how life's going to be different when I grow up."

Pg. 39

"Plant your feet on the seat. No one can see your shoes. Eat." Carlos stares at me like I'm crazy. "It works."

Pg. 44 escalates quickly from good time to fight then tattle to "Carlos has a gun." (shock)

Pg 51

"His daughter is studying me. I don't know why or how she sees me."

"He swallows, his tongue licking his bottom lip. 'I...' felt... threatened"

Pop get angry.

Stepping stones / old wise album people

Carloses gun is a toy gun

Pg. 64 fav quote: "I bet she doesn't even hear gunshots in her neighborhood." ✱

I realize now, the toy gun is what the officer saw. It is Carloses. Pg. 77

Pg. 95

Ghost boy spreads his arms and moves toward the window. It feels as if he's guiding me, like a gentle wind. Can Sarah feel it, too?"

"hundreds, thousands of ghost boys.

What the Hell!!! Not enough evidence? Are you serious? Pg. 138

Page 97 made me actually pull back and say wow, "Pain slams me. Two fire sticks are inside me..."

"Slayed crippled with grief." Pg. 100

Pg. 117 "Better to light a candle than curse the darkness."

Pgs. 130–131

"Why was the child shot in the back?" Officer, panic, stomping, cameras flashing, "No photos," as Sarah's the clerk. Reporters are shouting questions. Community activists are demanding justice. Ma, Pop, and Grandma... "I everyone knew this moment would come!"

Pg 141 – "how come life seems better now that I'm dead?"

All of Pg. 149 Emmett's whole story

Pg. 181 "... There ice blue, sparkling with tears."

Figure 2–11b Christian's Set of Important Passages

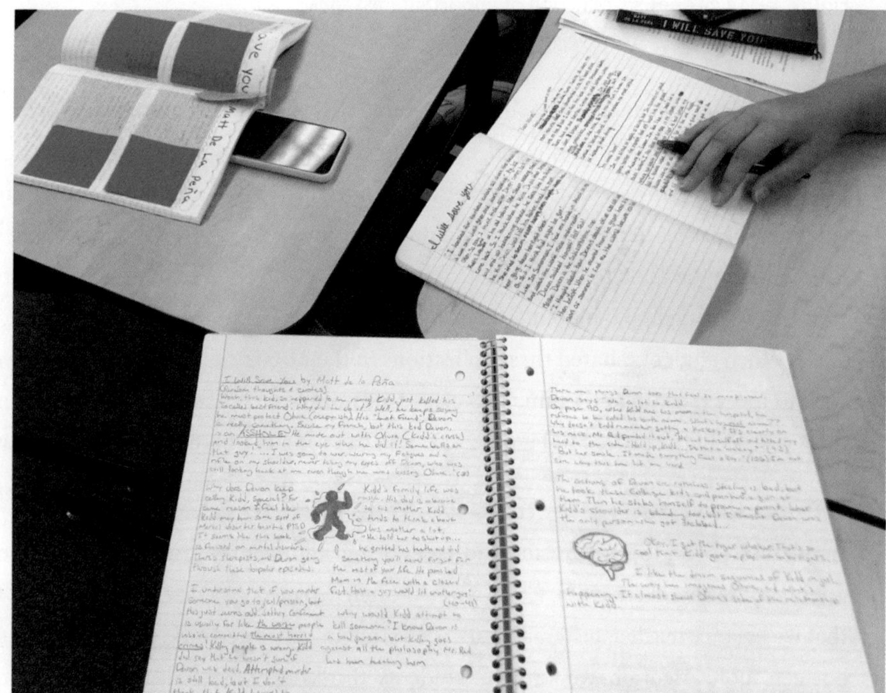

Figure 2–11c Students Share Their Memorable Passages with Each Other

a number of notebook entries, for example, we asked them to select one that interested them and to spend time deepening or extending their thinking during notebook writing time.

We gave our students a number of ways to extend their thinking in writing to fuel book club discussions. Here are eight of them.

Find a gossipy moment in the book: We heard Tom Newkirk say that literary analysis should sound like gossip. Instead of analyzing the work as a whole, the analysis should focus on a small moment and be anchored in questions like Why do you think that character said that? and Why do you think that person did this? We ask students to find and analyze a small moment that has large consequences.

Identify the turns in the book: We ask students to identify key places in the book where the story pivots. Can you put your finger on these moments? What led to these turns? Who in the book was most responsible? How did the author lead the reader to these moments?

Discuss a critical decision made in the chapter or book: We ask students to consider all the decisions made by people or characters and name one that had a critical impact. How was the rest of the story affected by this decision? What might have happened if this decision had not been made?

Capture a shift in your thinking: As a reader progresses through a book and new information comes to light, their thinking often shifts. To help them with this kind of thinking, we give them sentence starters:

> I used to think _______, but now I think _______.
>
> I still think _______, but I'd like to add _______.
>
> Others think _______, but I think _______.

Discuss a minor character of major importance: Often, minor characters are not minor. They serve a larger purpose. Though they may come and go quickly, their influence remains. We ask students to name a minor character who is a major influence and explain where that influence comes into play.

Pick a passage and read it the way the author intended it to be read: Considering how the author would want a passage to be read requires close reading. It asks students to pay attention to punctuation and nuance. It requires interpretation. Students practice reading their passages several times before recording them and posting them on Flipgrid for classmates to see.

Identify and discuss the most important word in the passage, chapter, or book: We ask students to select one word only and to explain the importance of the word in the development of character, plot, or theme. We collect these words on a chart, so that students can learn from the smart thinking in another group.

Annotate poetry: Sometimes we pick a poem that is connected to all of the books for students to read closely and annotate. This necessitates several readings, as we try to move students beyond surface-level, one-and-done reading. They discuss their findings in book clubs.

It's all about balance. Our students need to experience a high volume of reading, writing, and speaking, and they also need many opportunities to slow down and look closely at a text together.

Practice 5: We turn over decisions to students

These are decisions students make while participating in book clubs:

- Which book will I commit to reading?
- What am I thinking about as I read? How might I put that in writing in my notebook in order to prepare for in-class discussion?
- How can I best demonstrate my thinking in close reading practice?
- What does this open-ended question mean to me? How might I respond?
- How can I engage in Flipgrid conversations to both support and extend thinking in our book club?
- Which passages in this book demonstrate interesting writing craft to me?
- How can I respond to the finish-line questions? What matters to me in this book?
- What have I learned about an author's writing craft by reading across genres?

When students make decisions, they learn to be less dependent on the teacher.

Assessment and Grading

Before we start any unit, we ask ourselves what we want our students to take from the book club experience. For the social justice book clubs, we created this finish-line prompt for extended writing:

> Although students came from three parts of the country and different life experiences, we hope you gained insight into how others in our country see things differently than you do. How did this reading

experience change your thinking or give you new ways to see issues like #TakeAKnee or the Confederate flag controversy that have recently been in the national spotlight?

It is important to note that we gave this prompt to our students *before the unit began*. We told our students that to answer this prompt, they would be collecting thinking and evidence from three different sources: (1) the book; (2) the daily notebook writing we'd do in class; and (3) their interactions with others via Flipgrid and Google Docs. From these three different sources, students should braid their thinking to reach an insight gleaned from the overall book club experience. These essays served as their summative assessment.

Throughout the unit, we formatively assessed their progress through one-on-one conferences, their daily quickwriting in notebooks, their table-level and whole-class discussions, and their weekly self-generated two-page spreads.

Excellence in Essays on Author's Craft

In the Matt de la Peña author-study book club, we used the following criteria to frame our comments on the content of their essays.

Scope

Synthesize your analysis of the writing craft in the book and the writer's craft moves across other forms. Honor the voices of the texts, students in your book club, and you, the reader, in uncovering what makes this writer's work effective. Include quotes from the author's work as you develop your ideas.

Sequence

Organize your examples of writing craft by categories you design (e.g., literary devices, momentum, genre, beauty) and then explain how those categories contribute to the overall appeal of the work. Organize the flow of your essay to engage readers.

Development

Briefly summarize the novel as a context for the analysis of its craft. Use examples of writing craft effectively to support your claims about the writer's work. Evaluate the craft moves that engaged you in sustained reading. Anticipate and address a reader's concerns and curiosities.

Craft

Use word choice to create a believable, consistent voice. The voice should be tuned to explain, persuade, and address the reader directly. Literary devices such as alliteration and metaphor demonstrate your understanding of the craft moves you studied. Sentences have a rhythm that clarifies the message.

Editing

The essay is polished for effect (e.g., a balance of long and short sentences, intentional fragments, paragraphing decisions). The essay exhibits attention to and control of conventions based on audience and purpose.

Closing Thoughts

In book clubs, we saw our students' passion for reading reignited. This reminded us of a poignant story about reading found in Albert Woodfox's memoir *Solitary* (2019). Woodfox was a leader in the Black Panther movement in prison, and he followed its tenets to exercise personal discipline and self-sacrifice in service to others. When he discovered an inmate who couldn't read, he committed to teaching him. Once the man understood phonics letter by letter, word by word, he began to put words together. Woodfox says, "The first time I heard him read a sentence out of a book, I told him how proud I was of all he'd learned. He thanked me and I told him to thank himself, 'Ninety-nine percent of your success was because you really wanted to read,' I said. Within a year he was reading at a high school level. The world now was open to him" (230).

We understand the wisdom of Woodfox's observation: once students learn how to read, most of their increased proficiency comes from a desire to read. And yet, desire has been a sidenote in education for both students and their teachers for so long that perhaps we've forgotten what it feels like, what it looks like, or how its power can transform our schools. Passionate readers *make time* for reading. You don't have to force them; they arrive early to class with their books open. We've seen it. They don't forget their books at home; they ask for the next in a series. We saw this passion emanate from our book clubs. We heard it from a number of students who, after finishing their Matt de la Peña novels, asked if they could read another one.

Unfortunately, some educators have come to believe we are not responsible for desire, interest, or motivation. "That's the parent's job," they tell us. "I can't help where they come from." No one argues with this—we can't change what happens outside the school day. But a reader's interest in reading cannot be dependent on the home they left that morning. *We* own this. What happens in our classrooms has an enormous impact on what readers do when the school day ends. What if, instead, we aligned all of our resources to inspire every student during the school day to want to read more?

Instead of rushing to teach every ELA standard, what if we adopted only the five minimalist standards advocated by educator and author Mike Schmoker? What if we measured growth by the following criteria?

- the number of grade-level knowledge-rich books read in a year
- the number of pages of actual texts read per year
- the number—and approximate length—of inquiry-based discussions of texts per week
- the number of brief, formative written assignments per week, in every course
- the number—and approximate length—of formal, multiparagraph or multipage written assignments per course (Schmoker 2020, 48)

These are the first steps. If our students haven't met them, what is the benefit of moving forward? Schmoker recommends sixty minutes of reading each day *in school*. This means we need bigger chunks of time to read in our classes and in the content areas in order to combat the forces outside of our classrooms. This means we need more time to confer with our readers. And if we adopted these standards—if our goal were truly focused on developing lifelong readers—our lessons would be less about skills and strategies to pick apart the Great American Novel. We would deeply understand that helping a student find a passion that inspires them is the first goal. And if this goal really became second to none, book clubs would rise in prominence.

Students need voluminous reading before they get to college and the workplace. If we are strategic in how we set book clubs up, our students will be much more likely to find reading satisfying. And when they move away from the act of reading as performative scholarship and start reading because they are genuinely interested, reading volume increases dramatically. This, in turn, helps them to generate their own thinking and to sharpen their decision-making skills. With increased volume comes complex thinking across texts. The reading they do in book clubs thus becomes a critical part of their strength and conditioning training.

Donald Murray once said that the best teacher of writing is the writing. It is not the teacher. It is not the teacher's instructions. It is not the test. The best teacher of writing is the writing you do. It is the drafts in different genres. It is the brainstorming, drafting, revising, sharing, and tinkering with words to make writing worth reading by others. *The best teacher of writing is the writing itself.*

If we may be so bold, we might take Murray's idea and suggest that the best teacher of reading is the reading. It is not the teacher. It is not the teacher's questions. It is not the literary analysis essay. The best teacher of reading is the reading you do. It is the reading of different authors and genres. It is the wrestling with ambiguity, the predicting, the visualizing, the questioning, the evaluating, the reflecting, the revising of understanding, the connecting to your prior knowledge and background, the inferring—all these moves you acquire when you read a lot. *The best teacher of reading is the reading itself.*

If that's true, then our first job is to get kids to *really* read. A lot. Creating book clubs around provocative books does more to get our kids to read than anything else we do. It is our number one tool. To illustrate this, we will close this chapter by sharing brief anecdotes about three of our students, Ernie, Andrew, and Mackenzie.

Ernie entered twelfth grade not having read a book since reading *Captain Underpants* in the sixth grade. That's right—six years without reading a single book. Reconnecting Ernie with books proved a challenge, as he had become an expert fake reader. Someone who hated reading. A serial abandoner of books. You know Ernie, don't you? We can feel you nodding your head in affirmation. We all have Ernies sitting in our classrooms.

But then, one day, when hope was almost lost, Ernie started reading. Really reading. What changed? Ernie "met" Matt de la Peña. He selected *We Were Here* to read in a book club and, suddenly, Ernie was all in. *We Were Here* is the story of a teenager who has been in and out of juvenile hall and who has lived in group homes, and as it turns out, Ernie was a teenager who had been in and out of juvenile hall and who had lived in group homes. Ernie recalled, "I thought the book was really interesting. I could relate to a couple of parts in the book where the boys were in a group home. I was in a group home myself, so I know myself what it is like to be stuck in that position where you really can't do nothing about it." When Ernie arrived in his weekly discussion groups, *he had things to say.* (He never felt this empowered when we studied *Hamlet*—even though Kelly teaches the hell out of that play.) Immediately after finishing *We Were Here*, Ernie selected and read another de la Peña novel. From there, he picked up Danielle Paige's *Dorothy Must Die*, the first of six books in a series. When he finished that book, he asked Kelly for the next one in the series.

Sitting one table over from Ernie was Andrew, whose group was reading de la Peña's *Mexican WhiteBoy*. Andrew was a shy young man who rarely said much in class, but he really came out of his shell during the book club discussions. In a Flipgrid posting he shared between schools, Andrew said that reading *Mexican WhiteBoy* was a "godsend" because he had never read a book before about a character who was half-Mexican and half-white (Andrew is half-Mexican and half-white). When was the last time a student told us that a book was a godsend?

We also think of Mackenzie, who wrote the following after reflecting on his reading of *There Are No Children Here*:

> I had never been in a book club before. I had never experienced poverty before. And I had never known the meaning of equity before. All of that changed when I began reading *There Are No Children Here* by Alex Kotlowitz. I don't mean this in a way that is going to help support evidence from the book and make it easier to write this paper. I mean, in an honest and sincere way, that reading this book while participating in an across-the-country book club changed my outlook on equity in the United States.

Reading the book changed his outlook on equity in the United States. We love this, for we believe that the reader who exits a book should be different from the reader who entered the book.

Clearly, for Ernie, Andrew, and Mackenzie and many of their classmates, it was the book club experience that opened the reading door. It was opened because they could choose what they wanted to read from a list of contemporary, high-interest books. It was opened because their reading wasn't smothered by chapter quizzes. It was opened because they had multiple opportunities to wrestle with their thinking and experiences with others in small groups. And it was opened because they saw themselves and others in a different light. That is the power of book clubs. They position our students so that the actual reading becomes the best teacher of all.

POETRY

The Potential for Unexpected Things

Can we be honest? We have often struggled with ways to teach poetry. We've tried teaching it the way it was taught to us in high school: one classic poem plus a classroom of students equals analysis, analysis, analysis. We've tried reading and writing next to poems throughout the year, like we shared in *180 Days* (Gallagher and Kittle 2018). We even tried teaching form after form (cinquain, sonnet, haiku), which kept students busy but resulted in stale, flat writing. And if we are really being honest, there are times when we avoided the teaching of poetry completely. Because neither of us is a poet, we felt inadequate.

We have come to realize we are not inadequate. Neither are you. We have shifted our thinking, which is best summarized by the poet Naomi Shihab Nye:

> There's something that happened with poetry along the way where people started thinking of a measurable substance—you get it or you don't get it. Just sweep that out of the room, and create a sense of love. What you don't need for the teaching of poetry, I think, is to feel as if you're an expert . . . but you do have to find places of real love within yourself, for lines, for topics, for ways of writing, for styles that help you create a mood, an atmosphere where poetry becomes contagious. (in Alexander 2019, 29)

We can do that. We can sweep out the old notion that poetry must be taught as a measurable substance. There is no rubric for a great poem. The love of poetry has been dormant for too long. We must reawaken its power. As professor Thomas C. Foster notes, poetry "offers a window into the human experience. . . . That's what we want, right? Love, hate, envy, elation, dejection, gentleness, the mysteries of life and death, handled in a small package" (2018, 6). We love these small packages, and we want our students to love them as well. *This is important to us*, a key part of our mission as English teachers. Like us, what teenager is not interested in love, hate, envy, elation, dejection, gentleness, and the mysteries of life and death?

Poems are little mysteries. We are afraid we will not hold all the "correct" answers, and this makes us vulnerable. And for students, wariness is often rooted in the feeling they are "somehow overmatched, as if it were a contest and the other side had better equipment and more skill" (Foster 2018, 3). There is an irony here: teachers and students resist poetry, even though poetry exists in all of us. As a result, poetry has been devalued—and in some cases outright ignored—in many ELA classrooms.

This missed opportunity is tragic. A poetry unit is as important as an essay writing unit or a book club experience. In *180 Days*, we shared how we used poetry across the school year to spur student writing, but looking back, we now realize our approach came up short. Yes, our students read a lot of poems, but we used these poems to augment other units. Poetry deserves its own study. An English course without a poetry study is analogous to a mathematics course without the study of multiplication.

We believe the ability to elevate poetry to its proper place lies in our hands. This means not only bringing poetry back to its prominent place in the curriculum but also reimagining the way poetry is often taught. Instead of starting with the goal that all students will be able to deeply analyze a handful of poems selected by the teacher, we begin with a different vision: that all of our students will develop a hunger to read and write poetry. And when we start with this as our vision, everything changes.

Our Beliefs About Teaching Poetry

Belief 1: Poetry units are taught upside down

We have all seen the food pyramid—the USDA's former guidelines in graphic form for what and how much you should be eating. You are supposed to eat the most of what is at the bottom, widest part (vegetables)—and the least of what is at the top (sweets). Now consider what this pyramid might look like if we replaced food items with the ways we want to teach poetry. In other words, the largest part of the pyramid would represent what we do the most. We suspect the *traditional* teaching of poetry might look like the pyramid in Figure 3–1.

We have both been students in classes like this, and we developed an uneasiness with poetry. This can be traced to two problems: First, reading a poem and annotating it and then reading another poem and annotating it turns the study of poetry into a series of assembly-line tasks. We are not interested in piling on analytical practice at the cost of creating students who

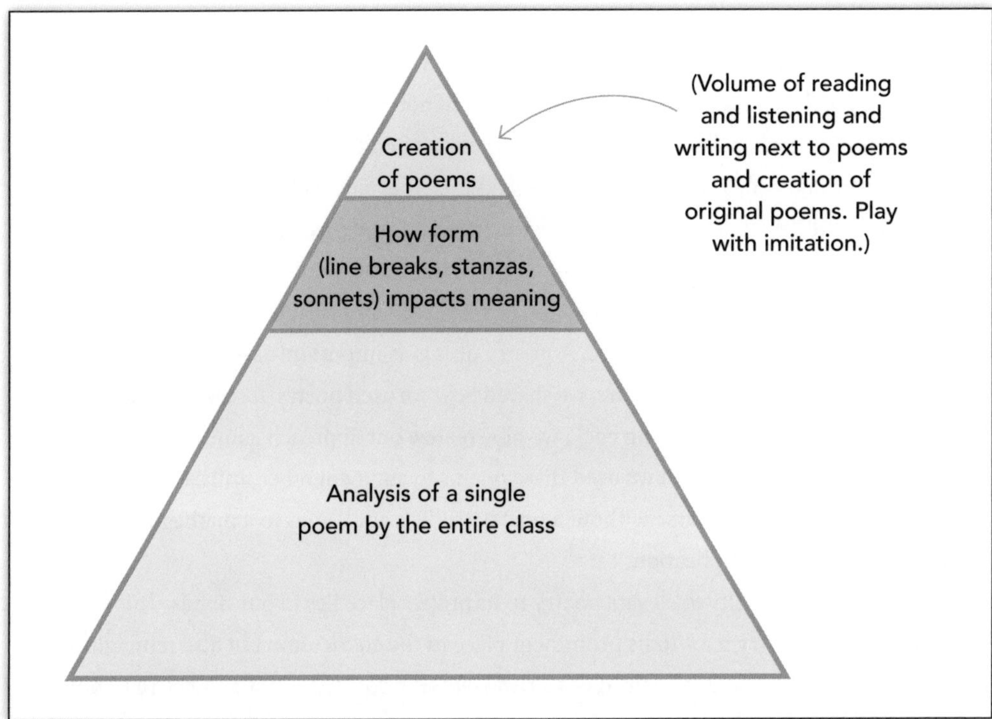

Figure 3–1 Traditional Poetry Pyramid

dislike poetry—that's far too high of a price to pay. And second, we believe rigor and true engagement arise from something deeper than analysis—the act of creation. It is one thing to read and understand a poem. It is something else to write one. We want our students to create because it is creation, not analysis, that generates the richest thinking human beings do. This was noted by a group of cognitive psychologists, curriculum theorists, and instructional researchers who revised Bloom's taxonomy in 2001. They placed *create* at the very top of cognitive challenges (Armstrong 2010).

We believe the pyramid in Figure 3–1 is upside down. Instead of grounding our unit in analysis and literary criticism, we fill the widest part of our poetry curriculum with reading, listening, and creating: standing immediately on the shoulders of poets. We start with playing, wondering, freewriting, reading and listening to poems, creating notebook lists and phrases, and imitating (see Figure 3–2).

This difference in our regular practice is important: quickwriting is not focused on analyzing a poem, but rather on how the poet's words help our students access experiences that they

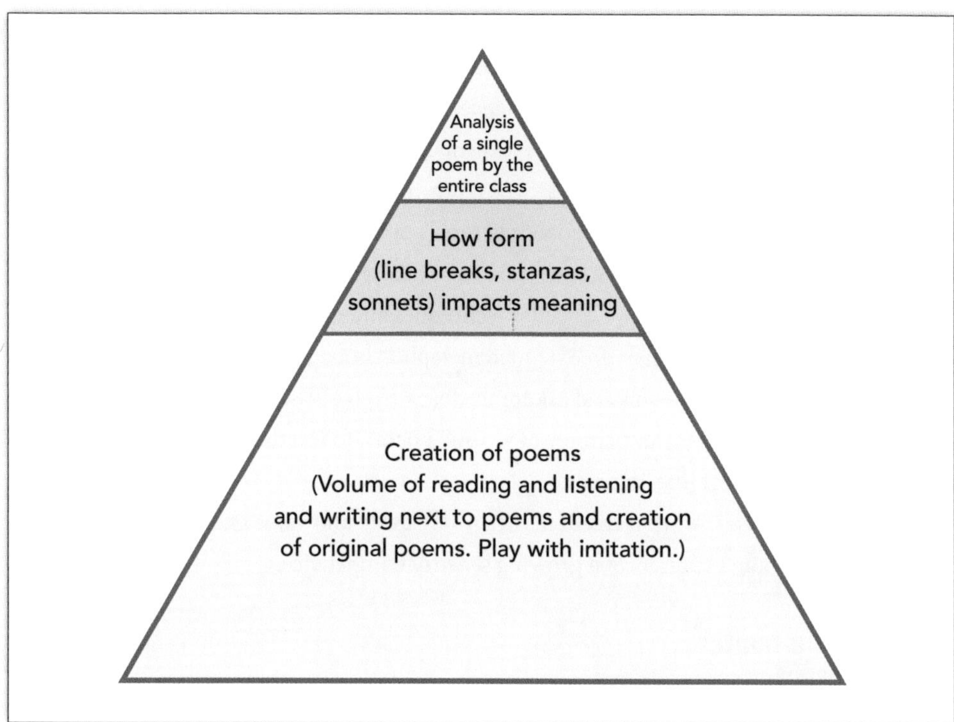

Figure 3–2 Our New Pyramid on the Teaching of Poetry

want to write about. Students, like all humans, seek meaningful connections with others. For this to happen, we allot far more time for creating and sharing poems.

Perhaps you think students who enter high school have already had sufficient practice with writing poetry and thus are ready for a unit steeped in analysis. Not true. Writing poetry is as neglected in elementary and middle school as it is in high school. Why might that be? One answer: we avoid what we do not feel confident to teach. Most teachers don't write poems and don't intend to. If we, their teachers, don't write, we bring all of our reluctance to our study. But if we want to break through student reluctance, we must break through our own reluctance. We must struggle, in front of our students, to model how poems arise from ordinary experiences.

And yet, there is another reason a shift in teaching priorities may be hard for teachers: the pressure to prepare students to analyze poems on standardized exams. But this kind of analysis practice in the classroom feels to us like planting neatly aligned rows of corn—a standardized approach where the students practice planting row upon row, all the same. Students look at the same poem and come up with the same analysis in a discussion led by the teacher, who likely is influenced by an analysis written in a teacher's guide. This repeated practice allows students to ride the wave of the thinking of others, without truly being connected or engaged.

We want students to live in a poet's experience, to feel the moment with the poet, not to "know" a poem. In writing poetry, this means students gather ideas at a personal, not a standardized, level. They experiment. Take risks. Seek truth. They practice writing poems in their notebooks but will not be graded on the quality of their poems. They are rewarded for the quantity of trying. We sprinkle in analysis of some poems to raise possibilities for their own writing. We look at forms and patterns, and we consider techniques and name the craft moves we find. We imitate the power of repetition or an extended metaphor, but again, at the experimentation level. We share our beginning poems and ask for feedback from our students. Our goal is for students to discover the beauty and richness of writing poems, to feel that same sense of wonderment we feel when a great line emerges.

When the heart of our work is freedom, when we elevate and value experimentation, everyone in the classroom experiences a growing sense of competence.

Belief 2: Volume matters

Volume starts with the teacher. While we were writing this, Penny was reading Olivia Gatwood's collection of poems *Life of the Party.* She found something reckless and real that churns inside of Gatwood and lands on the page. Penny was up early to keep reading, to feel the energy of Gatwood's writing—coupled with her own need to put words on the page. She had no interest in writing *about* Olivia Gatwood; she wanted to write next to her words in order to find her own teenage self—her own recklessness.

We must find poems we are excited to read, study, and share. Poems that light a fire in us. The kinds of poems that when you wake up in the morning, you think, *I can't wait for my students to read these today.* Because of this mindset, we are constantly gathering poems. This is why we read collections of poetry as part of our personal reading lives. We collect daily poems through websites like Poetry 180, Button Poetry, American Life in Poetry, and the Poetry Foundation. We follow poets on Instagram. And this is why we ask students every year to recommend poems they love. If we are going to be excellent teachers of poetry, we must start by kindling *our* love of poetry. We will mix favorites from the past with fresh poems we believe will be responsive to this year's students. We do not use the same collection of poems every year.

Likewise, we want our students to read a lot of poems. Volume matters. Penny recently heard from Lorena, a former student of hers. Lorena, a high school senior, was lamenting to Penny that in her Advanced Placement literature course, they had just spent six weeks dissecting three poems. Each poem had to be color-coded six different ways (e.g., to show evidence of dramatic irony, to show evidence of extended metaphors, and so on). "I am dying!" Lorena wrote to Penny. She went on to say how much she missed being in a class where students had the opportunity to read numerous poets and hundreds of poems. We kill poetry the same way we kill core works. We overteach, and when we overteach, we kill the love of the genre.

Poets often speak directly to adolescents in ways we cannot. Reading more poems increases the odds that students will identify favorite poets. It gives them more confidence to dive deeper into the genre, and, more importantly, it provides them with ideas on how they may create their own poems. The more poems they read, the more comfortable they get, and the more likely they will feel that their experiences and ideas have a home in poetry. And while we set up conditions for students to read a large and diverse volume of poems, we also teach students to read poetry differently than novels. We invite them to linger. A collection of poetry is like a pile of hot rocks—it burns with intensity. Though we want our students to gulp books, we want them to sip poems.

Our students will not develop a deeper appreciation of poetry if they only read poems, however. They also need to write them. Penny learned this lesson in college when she took a poetry course. On the surface of it, the structure of the course was simple. Students had two tasks every week: they had to write each day in their notebooks, and they had to submit one new poem. These weekly submissions were read aloud in class and then discussed by the other students. This was the rhythm of the class. They would meet, the professor would select a student to go first, a poem would be shared and discussed, and then they would move on to the next student. The following week they would repeat the same process, sometimes in small groups, often as a whole class. At first, the idea of writing and sharing a poem each week was terrifying to Penny, but as the semester progressed, she became more comfortable. The more she wrote—and the more feedback she received—the more adventurous her writing became. And every week when she saw what other writers in the class were doing, she was nudged to try new things.

One morning the last poem shared in class was "Lipstick." Written and read aloud by a boy across the room, the poem raced from beginning to end in a rush of rhythm and rhyme. Its energy was contagious, its craft intoxicating. Applause exploded when he finished. He ducked his red face beneath a mass of dark curls as students stuffed backpacks. Penny walked to the beat of its phrases from Moreland Hall across campus to an intersection where she recognized a boy she had flirted with for weeks. The conversation that followed led her to her notebook, where "A Recipe for Flirting" emerged. She scoured cookbooks for phrases; she created a poem in a form she'd never seen; she revised that recipe for hours. In class the next week she *wanted* to read her work.

Looking back, Penny realizes she learned more about poetry in this course than anywhere else. This might come as a surprise, as it appears her professor didn't do much. After all, the students provided the curriculum; the professor "just" showed up and facilitated the discussions. He didn't even collect their notebooks until the end of the term. But while it would be easy to come to this conclusion, it would also be wrong. The professor's contributions cultivated writers. He set up a class centered on students producing lots of poems. He created a safe environment for young writers to share their drafts. He gave his young poets the freedom to create without rubrics or grades to stifle them. And in doing so, *he stoked a desire to think and write as poets.* Think of all the times in their lives where the ability to write a poem would be magical: weddings, Valentine's Day, funerals, Mother's Day, birthdays.

Belief 3: Teaching "the meaning" of a poem is problematic

> I read poetry every day and I don't "get" half of it. I usually find pleasure in my ear, or in an image, or a turn of phrase, but "getting it" is never my main concern because it's not always meant to be "got" in the same ways as other types of writing. Poetry is often about going out on a limb and enjoying the precarious position and potential fall. Teaching poetry should reflect this riskiness.
>
> **—Tim Staley, poet and teacher, "Unruining Poetry"**

Many years ago, in *Deeper Reading*, Kelly (2004) recalled teaching one of his favorite poems, Walker Gibson's "Billiards." Because Kelly wanted to reprint the poem, his editor had to track down Gibson in order to gain permission. After a long search, the editor finally connected with the poet. The editor recalls the conversation going something like this:

> **Editor:** The reason I am contacting you is to ask for permission for an author to use your poem "Billiards" in a professional development book he is writing for teachers.
>
> **Walker Gibson:** Why that poem?
>
> **Editor:** The author is a classroom teacher who has taught this poem to his students for years. He loves how your poem uses a billiards game to metaphorically represent the savagery of humankind—a savagery that is lurking just under the painted and polished veneer of society.
>
> **Walker Gibson** (*Long pause*): Hmmm . . . I never thought about it that way.

We like to think that Walker Gibson might have been pulling the editor's leg, but we are not sure. (To his credit, the editor resisted the temptation to ask, "So . . . then . . . what does your poem *really* mean?") This experience, however, reminds us that the meaning of a poem is open to interpretation. To be blunt, we are not concerned that the poet's interpretation may be different from Kelly's. A work of art—by its very definition—should be open to interpretation. We would never argue that a painting hanging in a gallery could mean only one thing for all people. Likewise, we covet different interpretations when our students huddle around a poem.

This, however, does not mean that there are no wrong answers when it comes to analyzing poetry. We like Sheridan Blau's idea that when it comes to interpretation, there is a ballpark of right and a ballpark of wrong. What's the difference? In the ballpark of right the reader can defend their interpretation of the poem by citing evidence from the text. Even though Kelly's interpretation of the poem may be different from yours (or the poet's), he can defend it by citing several lines in the poem. His analysis is grounded in things he can point to. Kelly has since shared this poem with numerous groups of teachers and has heard other interesting plausible interpretations. However, if someone were to step up and claim that "Billiards" was an attempt to criticize the president of the United States, it would be unequivocally wrong. The text does not support that. Just because we recognize that there may be a range of plausible interpretations does not mean that anything goes. There is a ballpark of right, and there is a ballpark of wrong.

But this was not how poetry was taught to us. We both recall sitting in English classes where, as Billy Collins laments, we "tie[d] the poem to a chair . . . and torture[d] a confession out of it" (1988)—all in search of the what-does-it-really-mean answer. We performed this act numerous times and then proved we could regurgitate "our" thinking into a standardized essay. We suspect this was what poetry study was like for many teachers, and we *know* it was like this for many of our incoming students. Poetry study builds wariness when the teacher always picks the poems to be studied, narrows students' thinking with a set of questions or a prompt, and standardizes the structure of everyone's response. Instead, we must let poems sizzle and simmer as we hear them, let the lines linger as we collect them in notebooks, and let the young poets in our rooms have their say as they stand next to poems and write into their light.

Practices Most Important in Teaching Poetry

We have identified six essential practices in the teaching of poetry: we begin with play, we have students contribute to poetry discussions in a variety of ways, we have students write poems, we teach the language of poetry, we ask students to immerse themselves in poetry study, and we require our students to publicly share poems.

Practice 1: We play with language

Our first goal is to lower our students' anxiety about poetry. To do this, we begin with wordplay. Specifically, we encourage our students to play with the words of other writers. This practice eases them into poetry. Here are six of our favorite wordplay activities.

Spine poems: Students collect books from the classroom library and stack them in combinations so that the titles on the spines make poems. Not only is this a fun way to begin playing with language, but it also helps students to become aware of the available books in the classroom library. Here's an example (see also Figure 3–3):

Heartless
New boy
Trickster
In my father's country
In the land of invisible women
God help the child.

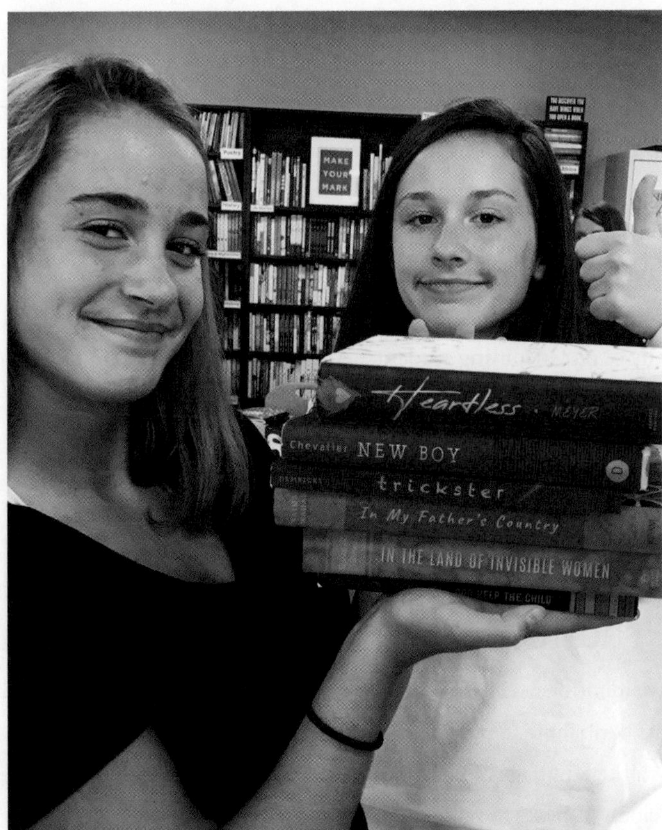

Figure 3–3 Liz and Becca Share Their Spine Poem

Found poems: According to the Academy of American Poets, "found poems take existing texts and refashion them, reorder them, and present them as poems. The literary equivalent of a collage, found poetry is often made from newspaper articles, street signs, graffiti, speeches, letters, or even other poems" (n.d.). We have taken students on a field trip, walking the halls of the school, to create a found poem from the language seen and heard on that short trip. We have had students create found poems from articles of the week, book club passages and chapters, or their own notebooks. We have also encouraged students to create found poems from combining lines across these works.

Another possibility is to ask students to find poetry within their independent reading. One student of Penny's wrote a two-voice poem (and recorded it with a friend in two voices) after reading *Gone Girl*. Emily created the voices of Amy and Nick using only the words from their chapters in the book. (See Figure 3–4.)

Blackout poems: In this activity, popularized by Austin Kleon in his book *Newspaper Blackout* (2010), students take a passage, and with a marker they draw boxes around words and phrases they will connect to create a poem. Once they have these words and phrases selected, they black out all the other words. These remaining boxed words are the poem. Unlike with found poetry, there is no rearranging of the words in a blackout poem.

Gone Girl Found Poem by Emily

Like a child,
I picture opening her skull
Unspooling her brains and sifting through it
Trying to catch and pin down her thoughts.

hold myself to him
Like a climbing, coiling vine
Until I have invaded every part of him
And made him mine.

She was funny.
She made me laugh.
And she laughed.
I'd fallen in love with Amy,
Because I was the ultimate Nick with her.
Loving her made me superhuman,
It made me feel alive.

Nick didn't love me, me.
Nick loved a girl who didn't exist.
He wants a cool girl
who is the girl who likes
Every fucking thing he likes
And doesn't ever complain.
Men actually think that girl exists.

Figure 3–4
An Excerpt from Emily's Found Poem

Lyric mash-up poems: For lyric mash-up poems, we ask students to pick a favorite recording artist and to print the lyrics to three different songs. They cut the lyrics into strips of individual lines and then mash up their favorite lines from the three songs to create one new song.

To build community, we might encourage students to work on these together. It is also important to note that we do not spend a lot of time on these—maybe a couple of days. Even then, we do not spend entire class periods on them. Alongside these playful activities, we also start bringing in a poem or two a day for them to read and write next to.

Crowd-sourced poetry: After the death of Ahmaud Arbery, an unarmed black jogger who was chased and gunned down by three white men in Georgia, NPR's *Morning Edition* asked for people's reactions in the shape of poems. They received over a thousand submissions. One of our favorite poets, Kwame Alexander, took lines from many of the submissions and created a community poem titled "Running for Your Life." Alexander, along with the show's host, Rachel Martin, then read the poem as a two-voice poem (Martin 2020). This powerful reading, which is available on the NPR website, is a good model to use to introduce the concept of crowd-sourced poetry.

There are two ways this idea can build community in a classroom. First, the teacher grabs a line or a phrase from each student's final draft of a piece of writing early in the school year and distributes these lines to all students. They don't yet know each other well as writers, and this reading aloud of fine writing craft from students binds the class together. Students work in small groups to rearrange the list of lines into stanzas for a poem. This draws their attention to voice and style. It isn't the product that is the purpose, but rather the time looking closely at the writing of others in the room.

The second way we have used the idea of a crowdsourced piece of writing is to ask a series of questions that students answer anonymously. For example, in Penny's Ghosts and Other Hauntings courses at Plymouth State University, she sent a Google Form to all students, asking for lines or phrases in response to these prompts:

1. Write a few lines that describe (in haunting detail) a place where a ghost might reside on the PSU campus. Find a place to write about. Imagine a ghost who might linger there or retreat to this place out of fear of all of you students.
2. Write something that a ghost who is sad might say if you could hear them.
3. Write something that a ghost who is evil might say if you could hear them.
4. Write something that a ghost who is lost might say if you could hear them.

After collecting answers, Penny combined them to create a setting and a haunting voice for the crowdsourced poem. She composed the poem live in front of students, talking through decisions around line breaks. She asked her students, "Should we break the line here, after *dark*? Or here, after *forest*?"

> In the overgrown, tangly, dark
> forest west of campus
> the ghosts of Plymouth
> seek shelter.
>
> In the overgrown, tangly, dark forest
> west of campus
> the ghosts of Plymouth seek shelter.

There is a tone of playfulness in this practice. Students like to see how their lines are interspersed with others, and it opens up opportunities for teaching about line breaks and the decisions writers make as they write and revise.

After this brief revision lesson, Penny used the crowdsourced poem to demonstrate voice recordings for students. She modeled pacing and clarity and moderating volume to increase tension.

Favorite lines: At the end of the poetry unit, we ask each student to review all the poems they read and to select one favorite line (e.g., you might have students collect beautiful words, phrases, and lines throughout the unit in their writing notebooks, like we showed in Chapter 2 for book clubs). Using heavy markers, you could write these lines on cash register tape and tack them to the walls of the classroom. Penny saw a similar collection when visiting Kelly's classroom, where student-selected lines from *Hamlet* were displayed everywhere. We work to surround our students with poetic brilliance.

Practice 2: We teach students to contribute to poetry discussions

Poems are great launchpads for all kinds of interesting thinking. To give students a sense of possibilities, we begin with an activity we learned from Sheridan Blau (2019), English professor at Columbia University. We ask students to study George Bogin's poem "Nineteen." After several oral readings of the poem, we write for ten minutes. During this quickwrite, students are asked "to contribute to a discussion about this poem." That's it. After students have written, we have them read their drafts to one another in small groups, and then we ask for volunteers to read to the entire class. While they are reading these drafts out loud, we chart the various approaches they took in the quickwrites. The last time we did this, some students

- wrote commentaries;
- responded to a line, word, or phrase in the poem;
- shared personal connections or stories;
- commented on the voice of the poem;
- analyzed other writerly moves;
- asked questions of the poet;
- analyzed the structure of the poem;
- wrestled with confusion in the poem;
- suggested the big idea through textual evidence; or
- made connections to other works of art.

As Blau emphasizes, there are numerous ways to contribute to a discussion. These varied approaches stimulate exploration, which makes the blank page less daunting. It encourages students to write because they have something to say. When students feel, however, that the teacher believes there is one correct interpretation of the poem, they move away from generative thinking and transition into performative mode. They dig in to find the evidence that will please the teacher. Blau, in *The Literature Workshop*, discusses the dangers that occurred when his students simply parroted his thinking back to him:

> As long as I was engaged in the task of teaching them what my efforts to construct meaning had yielded for me, all I could do was show them what I had learned. What they would know, therefore, was that I had learned it, and their notes would record some of what I learned. But the experience of learning was mine, not theirs. (2003, 2)

It is a theme throughout this book that we want to help students sharpen their own thinking by weaning them off an unhealthy codependency on their teachers' thinking. Blau cites Louise Rosenblatt, who once said that taking someone else's interpretation as your own is like having someone else eat your dinner for you. Blau warns that a steady diet of that kind "will lead not only to literary starvation but to a conviction that you can never eat for yourself—at least not the gourmet food served up in literature courses" (2003, 25).

Practice 3: We lead students to write poems

If teachers are going to guide students through the reading and writing of poetry, teachers must read *and write* poetry.

Yes, write poetry.

Don't close the book. Stay with us.

This call to write poetry may be a large hurdle for you. We know this because it was a large hurdle for us. We taught poetry for years without taking the crucial step of actually writing poems alongside our students. Yes, we were faithful in opening up our notebooks and writing narratives, arguments, and informational drafts alongside them, but when it came to poetry, we let our uneasiness with the genre get in our way. We both have advanced degrees, and we are published writers, yet when it comes to thinking about drafting poems in front of our students, we *still* get a bit squeamish. If we ever dabble with creating poems, we mostly do this in private, far away from displaying them on the document cameras in our classrooms.

We now know this was the wrong approach. Think of it in these terms: Imagine taking a class in filmmaking and finding out your instructor rarely watched films. Worse, he'd never made one. That would be unacceptable. This metaphor reminded us that when it came to the teaching of poetry, we had become the film teacher who never made films. If we want poetry to become contagious in our classrooms, we have to show students how we—their teachers—capture places of real love to write poems about.

The journey of a single poem

Penny called Kelly, and our conversation went something like this:

> **Penny:** I have been thinking.
>
> **Kelly** (*Very long pause. You should know that Kelly is terrified every time Penny utters those four words. He knows from experience that "I have been thinking" can often be translated as "We need to rearrange the entire chapter" or "Let's start over."*)
>
> **Penny:** Are you there?
>
> **Kelly** (*Warily*): Yes . . .
>
> **Penny:** You know how we believe we should do everything we ask our students to do?
>
> **Kelly** (*Warily*): Yes . . .
>
> **Penny:** I think we would gain important insight into the teaching of poetry by actually having each one of us write a poem.

Kelly (*Even more warily*): You want me to write a poem?

Penny: Yes, and as you write your poem, you can capture your thinking of what it was like to be one of your students. This makes sense as we will be asking our students to write poems.

Kelly: You want me to *write* a poem?

Penny: Yes.

Kelly (*Internally:* Oh, no!): Well . . . that is a great idea. (*Internally:* That is a horrible idea. I can't write a poem. I am not a poet! There is no way I am doing this! Ain't going to happen!)

It happened.

Here's how it unfolded and, more important, what we learned from it.

Writing session 1: Kelly began by searching for inspiration. He looked through his notebook, but nothing jumped out at him. In procrastination mode, his mind began to drift. He pulled up his calendar and noticed that in the next week, there were three different anniversaries: (1) the second anniversary of a surgery, (2) his thirty-fifth wedding anniversary, and (3) the first anniversary of the death of his mother. He was intrigued by the juxtaposition of these very different anniversaries.

Kelly decided to try to create a poem about the convergence of these anniversaries. He sat down to start writing and then proceeded to stare at a blank page in his notebook for half an hour. He eventually realized he couldn't start writing a poem by writing a poem; instead, he started by pouring his thinking out in prose first just to see where his writing would take him. Kelly started by writing about his surgery—about how healthy he is now and how grateful he is for his postsurgery experiences. He made a list of things he was grateful for, writing quickly to outrun his fear of not being able to create anything worthy. About halfway down the page, Kelly's thinking pivoted to the bad things he had experienced in the last two years (these experiences ranged from his mother's death to a global pandemic). Kelly started listing these awful things he had experienced, and it was during this pivot—this turn to the bleak side—that Kelly shut down as a writer. He did not feel he had the emotional bandwidth to go there. He stopped writing.

The next day, Kelly shared his progress—more like his lack of progress—with Penny. He explained to her that he didn't feel like exploring dark matters. Penny shared the thinking of the poet William Stafford, who said, "We play back our losses. This is the source of poems. A poem can be a celebration of loss. You can celebrate something you know is going to leave" (2003, 175). This got inside Kelly's head. He was intrigued by this idea. Kelly decided to revisit his list of dark events. One in particular—the recent death of his father-in-law, Richard—jumped out at him. Of the four parents of Kelly and his wife, Kristin, Richard was the last to die. Kelly was struck by the idea that when the last parent dies, the "children" (Kelly and Kristin) now become next in line. The baseball term *on deck* came to mind. Kelly wondered if that might be the title of a possible poem.

Writing session 2: Kelly returned to his notebook and wrote to the *on deck* idea. He drafted for a while but really felt he was going nowhere. Frustrated by his lack of progress, he returned to his initial anniversary-convergence idea for inspiration. This time he focused on the one-year anniversary of his mother's death. His mother had been comatose for some time, and Kelly was the only one with her in her final moments. He began writing everything he remembered about her last day, trying to capture all the details. Once this quickwrite was over, Kelly reread it to find inspiration, and circled the word *bruises*. (His mother had bruised badly.) He started to write about how the rapidly spreading bruises were an indication that her end was very near. It struck Kelly that his mother had suffered many "bruises" in her life, from the death of a daughter to a divorce later in life. Kelly started playing with the idea that although one set of bruises signified the end of her life, her death would release her from the many bruises she had been carrying for years. He envisioned "Bruises" as the title. Kelly started tinkering with the beginning of a poem, but after struggling for thirty minutes, he walked away from his notebook. It was late in the day, he was tired, and he decided it would be best to return to the idea with fresh eyes in the morning.

Writing session 3: Kelly sat down to revisit "Bruises." He wrote a bit but did not feel it happening. He decided to take a break. He picked up the latest copy of *The English Journal* and came across a poem by Todd Friedman titled "After Grading the Regents" (2020). But Kelly was tired, and as he quickly scanned the title, he misread it as "After Grading the Regrets." This misreading sparked a brainstorm: Kelly started listing his teaching regrets over the course of his career.

Kelly revisited "After Grading the Regents" with the idea that he might want to imitate Friedman's opening stanza:

> I wonder if God has committees
> who sit around a table,
> The Holistic Markers vs. the Sticklers.

Kelly tried imitating the beginning of the poem:

> I wonder if God keeps track
> of the mistakes I've made
> in room 905.

The simple act of writing those three lines triggered Kelly to remember a regretful incident he'd had thirty-five years ago with an eighth-grade student of his, Wallace. This memory—which came completely out of left field—sparked an instant desire to write. Kelly began drafting his memories of the incident. He worked for thirty minutes, then decided to leave it until the next day.

Writing session 4: Kelly returned to his draft. He knew it was terrible but was relieved that at least he had words committed to the page. He spent another hour shaping some of that writing into poetic form. Adding here. Deleting there. He wanted to give up and trash it, but Penny was expecting to see what he'd written, so he sucked it up and sent it to her. The caption of his email simply stated, "shitty draft/response welcome."

Upon receiving that email, Penny did not let Kelly off the hook so easily. She replied: "What kind of response would be helpful to you?" She was asking Kelly to do what we require our students to do: ask for *focused* feedback.

Kelly responded, "How to burn it? Anything you might suggest to make it better?" Again, avoidance. He had no confidence in the poem, so he had a hard time articulating exactly where he'd like the feedback. He deflected by asking Penny for any feedback that might help move the poem to a better place. How would you answer Kelly's questions after reading his poem?

Weather Report

In the beginning,
there was Wallace, an 8th grade tornado
whose mission in life
was to wreak daily havoc
in our 4th period English class.
One day, right in the middle of a classroom discussion,
he rose dramatically from his seat,
moseyed over to the wastebasket in the corner,
paused for effect,
and loudly hocked a giant loogie into the can.
Yet another battle line drawn.
As the class pivoted
to gauge my response,
I pointed to the door,
and sternly declared, "Weather report!"
Wallace knew the drill well.
He sauntered outside the classroom
where he stood, a lonely meteorologist, until summoned.
Upon his return, near the end of the period,
he walked to the front of class

and proudly announced: *"Lots of dark clouds,*
Looks like rain is coming."

That storm, like many others,
has long passed.
Now, in the calmness of its wake,
I have come to understand
that students who are the least lovable
are the children who need the most love,
that misbehavior is often rooted in trauma.
Instead, in my inexperience,
I made Wallace's pain a recurring joke,
and this morning when I think of him,
I want to reach back through time,
to pull him closer,
to let him know he is loved,
to let him know I see him,
to let him know I believe in him.
But since I do not know
where he has gone,
I am left
asking for his forgiveness
in this poem.

Note: Italics in the poem show the changes Kelly made after receiving Penny's feedback

Two of Penny's comments, in particular, helped Kelly to make his poem better. She wasn't sure if this battle between teacher and student was a recurring problem or a onetime incident. This prompted Kelly to revise the line to "Yet, another battle line drawn." Penny was also unclear about the transition between the two stanzas, so Kelly rewrote the opening to the second stanza. Penny also suggested adding a middle stanza as well, around the idea of explaining that Kelly regretted separating the student from the class instead of sidling up to him and trying to strengthen the relationship. Kelly wrestled with that for a bit but eventually set the idea of a third stanza aside.

Over the next couple of days, Kelly found himself drawn back to the draft. He continued to tinker with it.

We tell this story because it gave us insights into how we might approach the teaching of poetry. See Figure 3–5 for some of our insights, along with their implications (also available as Online Resource 3–1). We would not have discovered these ideas had we simply assigned our students to write poems. It's the *doing* that makes us better poetry teachers.

Insight	Implication(s) for Teaching Poetry
Find the right mindset. The moment Penny asked Kelly to write a poem, his immediate thought was, *I'm not a poet!* He experienced an instant surge of resistance. His fear was reinforced when he began writing and nothing "poetic" flowed. Kelly is an experienced writer, yet when asked to write a poem, he felt the same level of anxiety he did when Mr. Wheeler asked him to write one in his eleventh-grade English class. Panic.	Teachers can lower student anxiety by sharing not just their anxiety but their strategies to move past it. When Kelly felt paralysis creeping in, he took action: he looked backward in his notebook for ideas, he turned to writing prose as a way of gaining momentum, he abandoned several subjects he found he didn't want to write poems about, and he walked away until he felt like returning. We should teach all of these moves—and more—to students.
Live with uncertainty. The road to Kelly's best draft took many detours. He came to understand that he wasn't ready until he was ready, and it was important to not be overwhelmed by a lack of progress. Initially, he didn't want to take on a dark subject, but then the next day he found himself in a different frame of mind. It's interesting to note that the idea for his poem came when Kelly wasn't pressing to find an idea.	This experience taught Kelly that he hadn't done enough work with students on how to search for inspiration and what to do when that inspiration doesn't come. Ideas arrive on their own timetable. Uncertainty is normal. Poets learn to accept this as natural. It also reminds us that we can't expect all of our students to immediately find topics that will sustain them through several drafts.
Share with others. It took courage to share a draft. Kelly found it very difficult to ask for targeted response when he thought the entire poem was terrible. But feedback proved to be valuable at various stages of the process—it helped Kelly to get started and it helped him to revise. As part of that process, Kelly had to decide which responses might help him to improve the poem and which responses to disregard.	Teachers should recognize and celebrate the courage it takes to share writing with others. They should model how to ask for specific, targeted responses. Writers need encouragement, not criticism, and we need to show students how to respond to drafts in ways that help writers move forward. Once students receive feedback, teachers must model how to turn this response into meaningful revision. This revision has a more powerful effect on students when it is done in real time in class.
Find joy in the surprises. Kelly had completed many drafts before he made one key revision that dramatically improved his poem—he changed the student's weather forecast to a stormy day. (In his early drafts, Wallace reported that the weather was "around 70 degrees, a little bit of a breeze, not a cloud in the sky." Kelly changed it to "Lots of dark clouds, / Looks like rain is coming.") This single move shifted the tone to a more accurate representation of Kelly's intent: he wanted readers to understand this moment was stormy for him, even decades later.	That one revision move brought Kelly joy and energized him to spend more time tinkering with his poem. This breakthrough came as a surprise, as Kelly was already convinced that his poem was the best he could do. He was wrong. His decision to tinker with it one more time paid a big dividend. There are unexpected rewards awaiting writers who develop the tenacity to stick with their writing. We can't tell students this. We must lead them to experience this on their own. Teachers are most powerful as models of process, not product, and when we discover joyful surprises, we make them visible.
Free the writer. Kelly was grateful that he was not being held to specific elements found in a poetry rubric. It moved him from following a task to creating something for himself. There were moments, especially early in the process when he was having trouble establishing momentum, where the talk of grades would have had a paralyzing effect. He wasn't looking over his shoulder at the criteria; he had room to fail, to breathe, to experiment.	Students will be more prolific as poets without evaluation invading their thinking. When we tell a student that the finished poem must include two similes, a metaphor, and three other poetry elements, we not only box in the writer but strip them of the experience of making decisions. *Writing to a rubric is the antithesis of creating poetry.* (We say more about evaluation later in this chapter.)

Insight	Implication(s) for Teaching Poetry
Consider next steps. Kelly needed to decide if his poem was good enough or whether he wanted to work on it some more. As of this writing, he is considering eliciting responses from others. Even though Kelly did not follow his earlier "On Deck" and "Bruises" poem ideas, they are sitting in his notebook. He is considering returning to one—or both—of them.	We must give writers space to make decisions about their drafts, including whether to abandon them and start over. Teachers need to realize that the pacing will be different for each student, that poetry is not something that the entire class can write in lockstep fashion. A hard deadline for all poetry writers is problematic. (Which is true for all writing as well.)

Figure 3–5 What Kelly Learned About Teaching While Writing a Poem

One way to get yourself and your students writing poetry is to have them write next to other poets. To model this process, we watch Phil Kaye's performance of "Camaro" (2018). In this poem, Kaye wistfully recalls moments with a past lover. We annotate the moves he makes in the poem as invitations to get students writing. Figure 3–6 (also available as Online Resource 3–2) lists some of his moves and the ways in which students tried on those moves.

The Poet's Craft Moves	Student Imitations Inspired by Studying These Moves
Zeroes in on the details of a moment in time	Emily wrote of moments leading to her parents' divorce, ending with Dad standing in the doorway as he was leaving.
Writes about lost love	Our students wrote breakup poems, regret poems, poems of betrayal and unrequited love, and one proposal poem.
Last line begins: "I remember . . ."	Abigail began her poem with "I remember" and followed with a list in a tribute to a grandmother; Avery remembered the details of a car accident.
Begins with place: "You and I are standing at the Hertz rent-a-car counter . . ."	Brainstorming a list of places led to poems about former homes, working at Disneyland, cleaning hotel rooms, the dance floor at the junior prom, and a poem titled "A Story of Foster Care in Four Kitchens."
Links small events together to tell the story of a relationship	Adam wrote about being on the bus with a boy he liked on the way to a soccer game, catching his eye in the hall during passing periods, sitting next to him during an assembly, then holding hands for the first time.
Brings the past to the present: "months later we see each other . . ."	Kelly still imagines seeing Cindy Bayless, his crush in eighth grade, again. (Truth. Ask anyone who has been at one of our workshops in the last year.)
Uses an echo to bring the poem to closure: in the last stanza there's intentional repetition of an image or a phrase introduced in the first stanza	Mateo held his grandfather's hand as he walked beside him as a young boy and returned to the image of clasping his grandfather's hands at his bedside years later.

Figure 3–6 How Students Were Inspired by a Poet's Craft Moves

Practice 4: We teach the language of poetry

If you are a surfer, you know what it means to surf goofy-footed. If you like to knit, you might need to frog your knitting. If you are a waiter, you know diners will be unhappy when something is eighty-sixed. Every field has its language. Especially teaching. Could you imagine trying to make sense of the following if you were not in education?

> I was late for the IEP because my LMS froze when I tried to pull up the NGSS standards. I also need to remind myself that my ELLs will definitely need more SEL work before starting the STEAM program. Maybe we could discuss this in Tuesday's PLC.

Like teaching, the field of poetry has its own language, and to help our students acquire this lexicon, we provide them with the glossary of poetry terms found in Nancie Atwell and Anne Atwell Merkel's *The Reading Zone* (2016). Students analyze poems with more precision and confidence when they know the difference between an end-stopped and an enjambed line.

To help them learn the terminology, we start with a March Madness–style poetry tournament, an idea we learned from Penny's former colleague Joe Fernald. We select sixteen poems for the tournament bracket, and each day students read two poems matched one against another, with the task of deciding which poem should advance to the next round (see Figure 3–7 for a recent tournament).

When deciding on a winning poem, students must consider the technical skill (What are the moves and techniques employed by the poet?) and the affective elements (Does the poem touch your brain or your heart?). These two questions are related: if a poem moves you, it is because the poet has done something, and having numerous discussions around the "winning elements" of poems helps our students to acquire the academic language of poetry.

We have conducted these poetry tournaments for a few years, and here are some ways we have set up the brackets:

> **Page versus stage tournaments:** The first year we did a tournament, we set up the brackets so that one side consisted of page poems (just the text on pages) and the other side consisted of stage poems (filmed performances by the poets). We have found that the power of seeing a poem performed by the poet lends an advantage to stage poems over page poems, so in subsequent years we have created tournaments that focused on one or the other.
>
> **Thematic tournaments:** Penny's students once participated in a tournament that consisted only of Harlem renaissance poetry. Kelly once split his bracket in half to

Figure 3–7 Poetry Tournament

create an old school versus contemporary tournament. There are many engaging ways to match poems thematically—by poet, region, topic, genre, historical event, or era, for example.

Student-generated tournaments: Penny gave students a couple of days in class to listen to spoken word poems and to read collections by those poets, looking for entries for our next tournament. In doing so, students discovered a lot of great poetry, and having to winnow their discoveries down to sixteen poems for the tournament generated rich conversations.

Practice 5: We ask students to immerse themselves in poetry study

The poetry tournament is one springboard to sharpen analytical skills. We have also used the following activities to encourage close study. (We certainly don't do all of them in every poetry unit; if we did, our students would not have enough time to write their own poems.)

Poetry huddles (with thanks to Bob Probst, who taught us this strategy): In small groups, students tape a poem to butcher paper. At each table in the room is a different poem, often all by the same poet or within a theme. Students huddle around a poem, reading, analyzing, and annotating it. After a few minutes, each group shifts one table over and adds thinking to the poster the next group has left behind. The teacher circulates as well, adding their own thinking to each poem. We encourage students to wander and add additional thinking or simply read the comments written by others.

When we pull students back together as a class, we ask them to share what they found interesting in both the poems and the annotations. What craft moves did they notice? Which lines had the most power? Which conversation was most interesting?

These posters cover the walls of our classroom after the lesson. We are drawn to these student comments. It reveals what they know and what they don't know. We share examples with the whole class in the days ahead.

Interpreting history: The Mrs. Files is a 2020 series in the *New York Times* that explores what the honorific *Mrs.* has meant to women and their identity over time. Sarah Kay was asked to write a poem, "Mrs.," to introduce this collection of researched profiles. We love how this shows the multigenre possibilities with history and poetry. You might invite students to choose a famous war and write poetry from the point of view of soldiers on both sides of the war, as students in Penny's class did. Jonathan's "A Civil War Soldier's Lament" haunted her classroom for weeks after he read it aloud. You might take a current moment in history and ask them to write from different perspectives, perhaps in a two-voice poem. For some of our students, writing in someone else's voice gave them an entry into this form.

Poetry write-around: In small groups, students read a poem and quickwrite next to it. After three to four minutes of writing, students pass their quickwrites to their neighbor and respond to what another student has written. (We join this activity at one of the tables.) This rotation continues until the students receive their own notebooks back. Students then read the comments that all students in the group added to their initial thinking. Students discuss their observations.

Poet of the day: Over the course of a week, we feature a different poet each day as our book talk (e.g., Emily Dickinson on Monday, Rupi Kaur on Tuesday, and so on). We give students twenty poems from that day's poet to read during silent reading and ask them to select the three poems that generated the most heat for them. To help them with this sifting, we often ask, "What is this poet good at?" This prompts students into analysis as they make their selections. At the end of our daily reading, some students read aloud poems they chose. It is good for students to hear poetry read aloud by others and notice the decisions they make as they read (e.g., the emphasis on a word in a line; the pace of the reading). We stop and talk about these readings: "Why did you emphasize that word? Why did you pause there?"

Favorite five: We ask students to collect five exemplary poems from one poet. Angela, for example, picked her five best Sarah Kay poems and in a short analysis explained the rationale for her selections (discussing the technical and the affective elements). This spurs students to read a lot of poems, and defending their selections sharpens their analytical skills. When students share these findings, all of them learn more about poets and their work.

Thematic study: Students select poems around a theme or big idea (e.g., Jeremy selects war poems; Cassandra picks poems about social justice). In writing and in discussion, students explain why the poems they have chosen are important. They share their analysis of the craft of these poems.

Pairing poems: We give students two poems and ask, "Why did we pair these poems?" For example, we might hand them Phil Kaye's "Camaro" with Edwin Bodney's "When a Boy Tells You He Loves You" because they both explore the idea of love lost. Or we might pair "When in Love," by Marcus Jackson, with "Autobiography in Five Short Chapters," by Portia Nelson, because both are rich with metaphor. These pairings can be thematic, or they can be based on technical skill, or they can be both.

We never tell the students why we paired them. Instead, we ask them to discover connections. They often uncover connections we hadn't thought of.

Sometimes, we turn the tables and ask students to find two poems that are somehow connected. They bring these to their small groups and have their partners try to figure out the connections.

Punctuation study: Punctuation is not just used to clarify meaning; it is also used to *make* meaning. We have our students study punctuation in reading. Lena selected these lines from *The Living* (2013), by Matt de la Peña: "He shoved debris out of his way: splintered paintings, fallen statues, potted plants, jagged shards of shattered mirrors, chunks of ceilings and walls and stairs. Empty life jackets. Motionless bodies" (131). Here de la Peña is using punctuation to imitate the brokenness of the destruction left by a tsunami. His punctuation makes meaning.

The idea that punctuation makes meaning is certainly true in all texts but is heightened in poetry, where every mark adds extra weight to its intention. Consider these lines, for example, from Wilfred Owen's World War I poem, "Dulce et Decorum Est," where he describes exhausted soldiers returning from battle:

> Men marched asleep. Many had lost their boots,
> But limped on, blood-shod. All went lame; all blind;
> Drunk with fatigue; (1965, 55)

The men's exhaustion is certainly established through the poet's diction, but it is reinforced by the punctuation choices Owen made. He intentionally broke the flow of these three lines through the placement of two periods, two commas, and three semicolons. The reader is forced to trudge through the poem, thus deepening an understanding of the exhaustion the soldiers were feeling as they trudged away from battle.

Once we share this thinking with students, we ask them to find an important punctuation mark in any poem. Just one critical mark. Then we ask them to explain how this mark helps the reader to understand the poem at a deeper level.

Poetry autobiography: Georgia Heard asks students to find poems that define them. We love this. We ask students, "Is there a poem that captures who you are? Can you explain your connection to this poem?" Some students glue copies of poems into their notebooks and write next to them. Some combine the poem with a sketch or their annotations.

Poetry match: We ask students to match a poem with a person who should read it. "What poem do you wish your mother would read? Or the principal? Or the president? Why is this poem a 'fit' for this person? Why is it important that they read it? What insight might they gain from reading it?"

Beyond having students match poems to people, we also ask them to match poems to inanimate objects. What poem, for example, would complement their favorite song? (Kelly's former colleague John Powers used to teach Lord Byron's poem "Darkness," and as he read it to the students, he would play Barber's *Adagio for Strings* quietly in the background. The effect was mesmerizing, chilling.) In addition to songs, poems can be matched to movies, to paintings, to plays, to books, or to other works of art.

Poetry collection: Near the end of the unit, we ask students to create an anthology of poems. The selection process (Why is this a great poem?) requires students to analyze. They must include in this anthology a written reflection on how they selected these poems. This reflection can be a longer introductory piece to the collection, or students can write something brief about each selected poem. We encourage them to include their own poetry in this anthology.

Practice 6: We ask all students to publicly share poems

There are a variety of ways in which we ask students to share their poems with the class. Following are our favorites.

End-of-class share: We might ask students, "Who found a poem today that they'd like to share?" These are not necessarily their own poems. There is no other task attached to this—no note-taking or formal analysis. Students simply read great poems aloud. We like the notion of our students walking out the door with poetic language in their heads.

Choral reading: Here are two ways we have implemented choral readings:

- **Design multivoice poems.** Have students reimagine single-voice poems they have previously read as two- or three-voice poems. This means they recite some lines individually and some lines with others. To model this, we might have them start by looking at "Lost Voices," performed by Scout Bostley and Darius Simpson (2015; available on YouTube). Deciding how to read a multivoice poem is a challenge for partners or small groups. The line(s) recited by all students together must be of central importance. How will they decide on shared lines? How will they distribute the other lines? How will they perform the lines?
- **Choose your hot spot(s).** Prior to the choral reading, students read the selected poem and highlight their hot spots—words, lines, and phrases they find particularly meaningful. The teacher begins reading the poem aloud, and students join the oral reading only for their hot spots. For example, if nine students in the class had highlighted the third line in the poem, they would read that line aloud when the teacher got to that line. It can be insightful to see which lines receive the most attention, and it is surprising when certain students pick unexpected lines. The selection of their lines leads to vibrant discussion. Thanks to our friend Kylene Beers, who taught us this strategy.

In-class performance: Students stand up and perform poems live in front of their peers. We ask students to consider the moves of a good performance. We study a number of spoken word poets, and students discuss the speakers' intonation, pacing, volume, eye contact, and body language. We ask, "How does the performance elevate the poem?" Students choose to perform a poem they have written or a favorite poem by someone else. We've seen some memorable performances over the years. For example, one of our students delivered a poem about the death of a sibling. He turned out the lights and lit one candle in front of himself. As he finished the last line, he blew out the candle.

Flipgrid post: We create a public digital space on Flipgrid and ask students to record a reading of their poems and post them. For some, this is asking too much. Penny brought in masquerade masks for students to wear while they recorded. They can record someone else's poem if they are not ready to share their work in this way. Posting a poem motivates writers to spend meaningful time on presentation. This assignment results in a digital anthology of poems, and once students have posted, they spend a lot of time watching the performances of their peers. We love how this assignment reinforces the notion that we are a classroom of poets and how it encourages our students to swim in the poems of others.

Short film: Some students opt to share their poems publicly through the creation of short films. To prepare them for this task, you could start with an example like director Lez Rudge's (2020) adaptation of Georgia Heard's poem "Star Stuff" (available on YouTube). When we show poems turned into films, we ask our students to chart the decisions made by the filmmaker when it comes to imagery, pacing, lighting, narration, music, and captioning. We study other examples as well, including student-made films from previous years (see *How We Move* on https://pennykittle.net: click on Videos, then on Student Spoken Word Videos) and the famous Levi's commercial campaign called Go Forth, which includes Charles Bukowski's "The Laughing Heart" and Walt Whitman's "Pioneers! O Pioneers!" We have found this to be one of the most engaging assignments, and it is not uncommon for a student to spend twenty to thirty hours creating a film. Near the end of the unit, we celebrate with an in-class minifilm festival.

Public poetry jams: Some of our most engaged and adventuresome students have shared their poems at open mic nights in local clubs and coffeehouses. That experience led several of our students to join poetry clubs in college.

Regardless of the activities we choose, we stress the importance of memorization. Penny will never forget the time she and Kelly raced from gate to gate in an airport while Kelly recited soliloquies from *Romeo and Juliet*. Tom Newkirk said memorization "allows language to be written on the mind. . . . It is the act of owning a language, making it literally a part of our bodies, to be called upon decades later when it fits a situation" (2012, 76–77). We like the idea of having poems written on our minds. For the last ten years, Penny has recited "Days," by Billy Collins, to introduce quickwriting in class. We invite students to memorize poems, so that they can carry them with them for the rest of their lives.

Assessment and Grading

To examine the problems that are inherent when we try to grade poetry, Penny suggested that Kelly grade his poem that he shared earlier in this chapter ("Weather Report"). Kelly went to the internet and pulled a rubric from a nearby school district. This rubric valued five key elements: form, word usage, poetic techniques, language conventions, and effort—with each scored on a 1–4 continuum.

To grade his poem, Kelly started with the first category on the rubric: form. A 4 in this category states that the student "creatively uses an appropriate poetic form." Kelly looked at his two-stanza poem and wondered, *Is my form "creative"? Is it "appropriate"? What does that even mean? What does an inappropriate form look like? And who decides appropriateness when judging poetic form?* Seeking clarification, Kelly then read the 3 descriptor, which states that the writer "effectively" uses an appropriate poetic form (a step down from "creatively"). He then sat there staring at his poem, trying to decide if his form was creative or effective. Definitely not creative. Was it effective? Unsure, he turned to the 2 descriptor, which simply says the poem is in an "appropriate" poetic form. Kelly decided the structure of his poem was definitely appropriate, but as someone who rarely writes poetry, he did not feel confident enough to claim his form was effective. With a high degree of uncertainty, he scored himself a 2.

And this is where he stopped. (And we confess, as we read this aloud together, we couldn't stop laughing at how ridiculous this is.)

By scoring himself a 2 out of 4, Kelly realized the highest he could now score in this category was a 50 percent, which is an F. This did not seem right—if his form was appropriate, why was he receiving only half credit? (And it did not help that he realized that one of his favorite Emily Dickinson poems, "Fame Is a Bee"—a single-stanza, four-line poem—would have also scored a 2 on the rubric.) But it was not just the score that created a problem—it was the *effect the score had on Kelly's willingness to continue writing.* Having to measure the creativity and appropriateness of his poem—two extremely subjective measures—was deflating.

Maybe the problem lies in the rubric Kelly selected. He thought the same thing, so he went back to the internet and found more examples from other school districts. They all, however, presented similar problems. One awarded 20 percent of the score simply for an "effective" title. Another tried to quantify style. Yet another valued "poetic techniques." Kelly tried scoring his poem on a number of different rubrics, and every one of them had the same effect: they sapped his will to write. Remember the exhilaration Kelly felt when he had the small breakthrough of changing the weather in his poem from sunny to stormy? Gone. Getting a 2 on the first item on the rubric made Kelly feel wronged, hardly a motivator to keep going. No, the problem wasn't that Kelly had chosen poor rubrics; the problem is *all rubrics are poor rubrics.* They reduce a work of art to the measurement of specific features, but as we know, what the writing *does* is more important than the sum of its parts.

To move our young writers away from this feeling of being misunderstood, we adopt assessment and grading practices we hope will propel them to continue writing and revising. Here are some of these practices.

Assessment

The goal of assessment is to help both the teacher and the writer. The teacher assesses student work to inform instruction. We assess their drafts and ask, "What do these students need next? What should I teach tomorrow?" We make a list of observations.

When we sit beside individual students, we ask, "What feedback would be most helpful to you right now?" We skim drafts they are working on, assessing their progress while we listen to their analysis of what they need.

Donald Murray often reminded Penny, "If the writer leaves your conference not wanting to move forward with the piece, the conference has failed." We first offer students descriptive feedback: what a line made us think about, feel, or wonder. We look for ways we can nudge them toward more precision and clarity in their poems.

Writing groups

As we discussed in Chapter 1, when the writer directs the feedback, they are more likely to find the feedback useful. We ask students to turn in their drafts with a question, which requires them to determine what feedback would be most helpful to them in that moment (e.g., help with a particular section of a poem or feedback on a craft move they are experimenting with). When they meet in writing groups, they bring this practice to the group. Listening matters. The poet listens to the feedback of others and considers how to revise the work.

We've experienced the power of both support and too much criticism in our work. Penny was in a writing group of teachers at Kennett High School for more than a decade. These colleagues taught her the importance of feedback and gave her courage. She wrote for them and because of them. Over years together, they learned to ask each other, "How can we help?"

The feedback was most often helpful, but not always. Penny once wrote a poem following a visit to her brother's grave. She had never brought a poem to this writing group, so she was nervous. She said to her colleagues, "I want to know if you can see this moment." Her colleagues read quickly and jumped into a discussion of its technical aspects: "Why a line break here?" "Should this be two stanzas, not one?" "The title confuses me." They were all experienced poets, so this feedback was natural for them. However, there were so many questions and suggestions that by the time they finished, Penny was wounded. They never answered her request, so she believed her poem had failed. She had no energy to revise. She never brought another poem to her writing group. This experience confirmed Penny's belief that she should stick to writing prose.

Penny learned how critical it is to listen to a student's request for feedback. She now asks, "Was my feedback helpful? Did I answer your question about your draft?" Most of all, this experience reminded her how fragile writers can be when sharing work that matters to them.

Students' attitude about poetry

The most important assessment is this: Do students leave our poetry unit wanting to read and write more poems? To find out, we ask students to reflect on their interest in poetry at the start of the unit and again at the end. At the start, a survey like the example in Figure 3–8 (also available as Online Resource 3–3) will help us understand what they believe.

We have students revisit the survey at the end of the unit to notice changes in their attitude about poetry. Now most students can name their favorite poets. All have developed a practice for finding subjects they are passionate about. We hope they carry a love of poetry far beyond our classrooms.

Beyond the survey, we ask them to reflect on their learning. This will send them back to their notebooks. There may be a quickwrite they wrote early in the study that has promise. They may find a collection of poems by Blythe Baird that they had forgotten on their

	1 *never*	2	3	4	5	6	7	8	9	10 *always*
I enjoy reading poetry.										
I read poetry in my free time.										
I read collections of poetry.										
Reading poetry is hard for me.										
I read my own poetry.										
I write poetry.										
I like the challenge of analyzing a complex poem.										
I see myself as a poet.										

My favorite poets are ______________________________.

Figure 3–8 Poetry Survey

what-to-read-next list. They may be surprised by the volume of their writing. Or they may notice patterns in subjects. To help them name this growth, we ask them to reflect in their notebooks on the following prompts:

> **Reading poetry:** Discuss the poetry you have read so far. Name specific things you have learned. Use the poetry lexicon (the language of poetic craft) to describe what you have learned.
>
> **Writing poetry:** Look at the drafts you have finished during this unit and reflect on what your writing shows. What techniques are you trying? How have you revised a poem? After studying poetry for weeks, there should be evidence that your writing of poetry is improving. Name what you see in your work that demonstrates growth.
>
> **Recording poetry (reading aloud):** You have studied spoken word more than any other kind of poetry. One purpose is to understand how expressiveness, volume, clarity, and pace contribute to the audience's experience of the poem. You have completed a voice recording. Reflect on how recording your poem has helped you to understand the power of oral language and performance.

Excellence in Poetry: Grading Menu

We don't believe in grading individual poems, but many schools mandate that teachers post grades in all units. Given this reality, what follows is a menu of some of the ways we have worked grading into our poetry study. It is important to note that we do not have students do all of the ideas listed here. Why? If a student is going to create a quality digital project using an original poem as a voice-over, it takes weeks of time. We would rather a student do one thing really well than to try and cover every standard by analyzing one poem for days. Teachers (and curriculum designers) often default to analytical tasks because they are orderly and gradable: there are rules, terms, and ways to measure products. But writing our own poems demands more.

We don't have enough time to do many things well. So in choosing one from our menu of grading options, we would write beside the poems found in Porsha Olayiwola's collection *I Shimmer Sometimes, Too*, instead of analyzing her poems almost every single time.

Collection of original poems

Students collect, select, and reflect on poems they have written. They might, for example, rank five poems in order (most effective to least effective) and explain their rankings. In doing so, they consider the techniques they tried and the craft moves they used successfully. It is this reflection that we grade.

Each student turns in a poem for inclusion in a classroom anthology. We place these collections in the classroom library for dual purposes: as reading material and as mentors for our next poetry study.

Transforming poems using digital tools

Figure 3–9 (also available as Online Resource 3–4) explains how we scored one such project, the creation of digital movies.

Students practice sharing poems to close class throughout the unit, so at the end, we sometimes ask them to record and submit an audio version of one of their poems. We evaluate them via the descriptors of excellence listed in Figure 3–10 (also available as Online Resource 3–5).

Category	Elements to Consider When Transforming Poetry into a Digital Composition
Organization	Images, video, music, and voice-overs are woven to engage a viewer and communicate the content of the poem. There is a logical, effective sequence. The student brings closure to the composition (e.g., repeating a line or image, circling back to the beginning, or changing the pace).
Pacing	The pacing of photographs, video, music, and voice-overs maintains audience interest. Voice-overs are not too fast, not too slow. The pace is varied to align with the intentions of the lines of the poem. There is adequate time to read text slides.
Images	The images are visually pleasing and communicate the tone of the piece. Thought went into the placement of an image with those that come before and after. Shadowing and transitions might be used to ease the viewer from one stanza to another.
Sound	Music and video are adjusted for clarity and effect. A comfortable sound level is maintained throughout.
Editing	All spelling and punctuation is correct on text slides. Transitions are creative and do not distract viewers between sections of the video.

Figure 3–9 Descriptors of Excellence for Digital Movies

Category	Elements to Consider When Creating Voice Recordings of Poetry
Pacing	The pace is varied to establish and maintain listener interest. Avoid going too fast or two slow. Pauses create space for a listener to sit with the words before moving on.
Expressiveness	Express how you feel through your voice, sound effects, or both. Words and phrases that are most important are emphasized. Your reading has life.
Volume	Adjust the intensity of your words to match the content of them.
Clarity	Words are read clearly. The poem is read at a pace that allows readers to not just listen to the poem but absorb it.

Figure 3–10 Descriptors of Excellence for Voice Recordings

It is important to note that we do not score each category separately when using these descriptions of excellence for both digital movies and voice recordings. Instead, we look at each project holistically before assigning a grade. Students also know that no grade is ever final; if they're unhappy with their scores, they can continue to revise their projects to make them better.

Poetry analysis exam

In some settings, teachers are required to give an exam to close a unit. In Penny's school, it was required to be an on-demand essay. When giving a summative assessment, you might pick from one of these ideas:

- The class poetry tournament determined a winner. Write an essay where you explain why you agree or disagree with the selection of the winning poem. Use evidence of the technical and affective elements to support your analysis.
- Who is your favorite poet? Select an exemplary poem from this poet and explain why this poem is noteworthy.
- Pick three poems (written by different poets) that are connected thematically. Explain the connection. [We have students come to the exam with the three poems already selected.]
- Analyze the technical and affective elements in one of your poems.
- Discuss the evolution of a poem you have written. Share your insights as you worked through the process of writing a poem from initial idea to best draft. Discuss how revision changed the poem.
- Annotate the assigned poem. [We provide the poem, which might be a published poem or a student's poem.] Show your understanding of big ideas like theme, intended audience, point of view, diction, use of poetic devices, and how form impacts meaning. [This is an exercise they have done in small groups and as a whole class several times prior to the exam. When using a student's poem in class, we frame the analysis around this question: "What feedback can you give to this writer to help make this poem better?"]

We share the descriptors of excellence listed in Figure 3–11 with students prior to the exam. We also study one excellent essay from a former student who took the exam.

Category	Excellence in Poetry Analysis
Scope	Demonstrates a comprehensive grasp of the technical and affective elements of poetry. The analysis will demonstrate an understanding of the impact of writing craft on a poem's meaning.
Sequence	The organization of the essay has a clear purpose and a natural flow. It includes an enticing introduction, the use of effective transitions between ideas, and a closing.
Development	Develops analysis with well-chosen, relevant, and sufficient details, passages from the poem(s), or both.
Craft	Contains explanatory prose, mature vocabulary, precise language, strong voice. Skillfully integrates source and support material with commentary, using citations when appropriate.
Editing	Exhibits attention to and control of conventions throughout the essay.

Source: Adapted from the Puente Project, University of California

Figure 3–11 Descriptors of Excellence for Poetry Exam

Closing Thoughts

One semester, Penny had her students quickwrite to Patrick Roche's "21," a spoken word poem in which the narrator revisits the various traumatic stages of his father's alcoholism. For Lizzy, a college freshman, writing next to this poem led her to a topic she had never written about: the physical and emotional abuse she had suffered at the hands of her father. Like Roche does in his poem, Lizzy wrote of memories spread over the years, and the more she wrote, the more honest her writing became. This was something she had never written about before, nor had she shared this experience with anyone else. But there was something about reading Roche's poem that gave her courage to access and begin processing her deepest trauma.

Lizzy's story reminds us of something we read in *Reading Unbound*, where Wilhelm, Smith, and Fransen (2014) found that reading helps adolescents to develop identity. This is critical, the authors note, as the psychologist Erik Erikson argued that "the central psychosocial conflict of adolescence is identity role versus confusion" (92). Teenagers are trying to figure out who they are, and reading helps them to develop their identity in two ways. First, it helps them to identify themselves (e.g., "I am a Micah Bournes fan"), and second, it helps them to make connections (e.g., "I like to discuss Kwame Alexander's poems with others"). Noted psycholinguist

Frank Smith (1988) has written extensively about the importance of the social nature of literacy, citing how critical it is for young readers to feel they belong in the literacy club. Students who gain "admittance" to this club frequently interact with characters, authors, and other readers, and these interactions, in turn, greatly influence their emerging identities. But Wilhelm, Smith, and Fransen discovered something else as well—that the development of a *reading identity* can be one factor that leads to the development of a student's *writing identity.* Kids who like to read fan fiction, for example, are often drawn to writing fan fiction.

This idea of writing identity intrigues us. In our own writing, we often find ourselves returning to many of the same big themes. Some of these themes have spun from our reading, true, but not all of them come from there. Our writing identities have been generated by our life experiences. Penny often writes about her father's drinking, and Kelly returns to writing about his sister's struggles with addiction. These are more than topics we are interested in. They are deeper than that. They are events that have shaped our identities. Kelly's poem "Weather Report" is about teaching because being a teacher is a large identity theme in his life. Over the years we have both written about teaching a lot, and it is important to note that this writing has spanned a number of genres. We have written poems, essays, journal articles, blogs, reflections, editorials, tweets, and books all around the single identity theme of teaching. Our identity as teachers fueled our engagement with all of this writing.

We wonder if poetry has helped Penny's student, Lizzy, to discover what may become an identity theme for her—her history with her father. We have seen these deeper writing themes emerge in other students as well. Shawna repeatedly returns to writing about her mother's cancer. Damien is obsessed with writing about football. Estefana's notebooks are full of passages about her father's deportation to Mexico. These students are tapping into their writing identities, but it is important to remember that recurring themes are unlikely to emerge unless students are writing a lot in their notebooks. A volume of low-pressure and ungraded writing in response to poetry helps students to recognize these patterns in their writing. The intensity of poetry activates our memories and our imaginations, surprising us. It helps us to recognize those subjects that will lead to our most vivid writing. Once students have freely written on a regular basis, they can look backward in their notebooks and ask key questions: What subjects do I keep writing about? What's another way to think about this? What am I avoiding? And one more important question, which we believe has been largely ignored: Will writing about this subject work best as a poem?

In this poetry study, we asked our students to make many of the same decisions they had to make in the essay study. When writing alongside poetry in their notebooks, they had to choose their subjects, consider their audience, and think about their purpose. When creating their own poems, they also had to consider their forms, ask for targeted responses, use feedback to improve their writing, and immerse themselves in multiple revisions. This immersion in revision is the place we want our students to be. Noted poet William Stafford said there are two kinds of revision. He called the first "a kind of shuffling work, rational and reasonable at the information level" (2003, 136). We struggle to bring a subject into focus. And "then there's the revision where you feel the potential for unexpected things. . . . The muse is a feeling, a surge of energy. There's the drudgery of getting to the point and then you take off—you get excited" (136). The reason to get students into the habit of writing, he says, is because something might happen to them, "a kind of hydrofoil feeling" (135).

We want our students to experience this hydrofoil feeling, whether they are writing next to poems or creating their own poetry. Stafford names something for us that stands on other writers we've read and learned from: Anne Lamott, Ross Gay, and Dani Shapiro, to name a few. These writers invite us into a self-generating, joyful practice of finding and playing with and collecting ideas, then riding the wave of how those words might come together. We tell our own stories—starting where we want to—listening to them and asking, "Is this true?" We add and delete as we answer this question.

Writing practice with poetry is a gift for anyone. We recognize, however, that most students are not going to take a course in poetry at the college level, which is why we feel an added responsibility to bring the joy of reading and writing poetry into their lives. It is not hyperbole to say that for many of them, gaining an appreciation of poetry is now or never. We are saddened by the idea that many of them have not discovered the joy of writing their way into "unexpected things." A vibrant poetry study can change this.

The poet Jericho Brown said, "Hope is always accompanied by the imagination, the will to see what our physical environment seems to deem impossible. Only the creative mind can make use of hope. Only a creative people can wield it" (2012). We love this connection between creativity and hope. It reminds us of the importance we play in fueling our students' inventiveness and imagination. With this in mind, we finish this chapter with the words of Jeff Tweedy, lead singer of Wilco: "If a song is conjured more than it's crafted with intent, why have we been learning all these exercises, doing all the work step by step? Because hopefully all of what I've been sharing here is in service of reconnecting with your imagination in a way that will eventually allow you to just close your eyes and imagine what comes next" (2020). Though Tweedy was talking about songwriting, his thinking applies to the reading and writing of poetry as well. For shouldn't this be our primary mission—to reconnect our young writers with their imaginations? Don't we want them to close their eyes and imagine what comes next?

DIGITAL Composition

Crossing Genre Boundaries

> The problems and solutions of writing with clarity and grace cross all genre boundaries.
>
> —**Donald Murray,** *Learning by Teaching*

shley is studying her computer screen, headphones in, while the rest of fourth block jostles and gossips in the last minute before class on a blustery Monday. Penny sees Ashley's time line for her documentary open before her and watches as she cuts one-tenth of a second from a video she has lifted from ESPN for the introduction. As the bell rings, Penny drops her hand to Ashley's shoulder, and she startles, removing her headphones.

"Tell me what you're doing." Penny nods to the screen.

"Oh." Ashley smiles. "I'm using footage from Sochi in the opening. I was just cutting it." She explains that this ten seconds of ski racing, which would show us the subject of her documentary, was taking her hours to edit. She wanted it to be just right. "See, my title will appear after this—like the one we saw in a movie you showed Friday."

"It's beautiful work," Penny tells her. "How long have you been working on your movie?"

Ashley studies the screen. "Seriously, Mrs. Kittle, just the first thirty seconds or so has taken me about ten hours of work this weekend." She tucks her head, and glances around the room. She is in a mixed class of grades ten through twelve, and as one of the youngest students in the room, she doesn't want to be seen as a teacher's pet or a try-hard. But she doesn't need to worry. Now that we've turned our attention to digital composition, they are all try-hards.

What is it about digital composition that changes teaching and learning? So many things: the opportunity to create—the wide-open world of possibility and vision; the natural collaboration that emerges as they share bits of their movies with each other and listen to feedback; the curiosity they feel to not just consume media but also understand how it is created. And a fundamental truth: they know more about this than their teacher does. Students are faster to learn the tools they need and eager to experiment. Revision is a natural part of the process. As the classroom shifts to a place of collaborative, shared learning and productive talk, time gallops by.

Of the four units in this book, three are likely familiar to you: book clubs, essay writing, and poetry. We hope we have given you new ways to consider those studies, but it is unlikely that our thinking on those subjects has upended you. This unit might. Stay with us: we've stumbled along ourselves in learning how to lead students to create in digital media, but it has always ignited energy in our classrooms. Digital composition is where relevance and rigor meet.

Our Beliefs About Teaching Digital Composition

Belief 1: Digital composition is not just engaging; it is necessary

Even before the worldwide pandemic of 2020–21, students were consuming more media than ever before. In 2019, American teens, ages thirteen to eighteen, used entertainment screen media for seven hours and twenty-two minutes each day (Smart Social 2020). Then the pandemic struck, and the effects of isolation on social media were immediately seen. Consider the following:

- "Video-streaming platforms have seen over 113 percent rise in the number of average users since the nationwide lockdown" (Gupta 2020).
- "The surge in the use of social media platforms has been estimated at 82 percent as it became the primary medium of communication and entertainment during the lockdown" (Gupta 2020).
- "The screen time spent on social media will continue to grow as the users are posting 352 percent more content, and are spending an average 4 hours on the apps as compared to 1.5 hours previously" (Gupta 2020).

There will be no going back, postpandemic. It is not an accident that YouTube, Instagram, and TikTok—all platforms that use video—are the most used social media apps by teenagers (Smart Social 2020). Whether students are interacting with friends, entertaining themselves, or searching for news, digital texts have become central to their lives.

We know that the best way to become a critical thinker about digital media is to create in that genre. You may recall in Chapter 3 that when we wanted our students to understand poetry, we had them create poetry. The same principle holds true here as well—if we want kids to understand and analyze digital compositions, we must guide them in creating digital compositions.

Belief 2: Composition is composition

Early one September, Penny began talking through a presentation for NCTE with Matt Glover, a brilliant thinker in literacy. Matt's theory was that success with one literacy can lift another, and he shared a video of preschool girls acting out stories. The three- and four-year-olds were composing complex stories, but their tools were not pen and paper. The practice in oral storytelling allowed them to develop their ideas without the constraint of written conventions. Penny and Matt believed this idea was bigger than preschool. In fact, Penny has since named this theory Oscar.

Oscar was tall, good-looking, polite, and serious, but on the first day of his college composition class he confessed he never read and that he resisted writing anything. He knew he was unprepared for college writing and increasingly worried he'd never master it. He told Penny that in high school a tutor had outlined essays and coached him in writing them. He ducked his head when he admitted that she'd even written his college admission essay. Now, as a freshman, he avoided, resisted, and stumbled over written essays in all of his courses.

Oscar was a skilled running back on the football team, so Penny suggested he needed an end run around genre. Instead of having him write a draft, she asked him to consider recording a draft to take advantage of his natural storytelling ability. She advised that he listen to a podcast series instead of reading mentor texts. Sometimes we can help students to circumvent difficulty by opening up the writing process through new possibilities. This is what Oscar did.

Instead of writing, he used a combination of sound effects and clear observations of a cemetery to create an engaging voice recording for his writing group meeting. The language in his recording was clever and shrewd, and as he watched the faces of students huddled together with earphones in, he thought, *I'm* good *at this*, which surprised him. Penny suggested he begin all first drafts this way. Oscar learned to let his thinking wander and coalesce as he walked across campus, using his phone's voice recorder to take down his thoughts. Later, he transcribed his recordings into essays. Digital literacy was an essential bridge to establish Oscar's identity and confidence as a writer. In his final course evaluation he said, "I have never been a reader. I just never found a book that speaks to me. I hate writing. But the voice recording was the best thing I've ever done."

Yet in school many students practice composition in only one medium: written text. We know it is the form privileged by standardized tests, but our goal is not to create good test takers; we want thinkers and creative composers. An argument poem (e.g., Gibson's "America,

Reloading"; see pages 9–10) gains power when lifted from the page to be read by the author in a movie rich with images. Anything students have already written has similar digital possibilities. It is not uncommon for students to tell us that it is exhilarating to take written words and turn them into a visual or audio composition.

Likewise, digital composition is uniquely positioned to support multilingual learners in their process of composing thinking. "Writing is writing regardless of the language," argue Cecilia Espinosa and Laura Ascenzi-Moreno in their terrific book *Rooted in Strength* (2021). They say, "Although cultural and language-specific conventions exist, the construction of meaning is at the heart of writing" (144). Students learning a language have ideas that often jump ahead of their written language acquisition. Composition is composition, and our teaching must reflect that. We are not abandoning written texts; rather, we know that composing in another medium will lift that written work for many of our students.

Belief 3: Teachers must overcome the fear factor

David Sousa, noted expert on brain research, reminds us that two things have to be present before deep learning can occur: structure and novelty (2001, 27). We have to have structure in our classrooms, Sousa says, because students cannot learn in chaotic environments. But structure alone is not enough. We must also create novel opportunities for students to learn. The brain is a novelty seeker.

This thinking applies to teachers, as well. We like structure. We find comfort there. If it's April, it's time for our four-week poetry unit. Planning the year gives us one less thing to worry about. And let's face it, it would be easy to continue to teach the same units year after year. But we must also remember that novelty is good for us as well. Yes, the thought of doing something new and unproven is scary. And yes, it may raise your heart rate and anxiety a bit. But novelty is not just essential for student growth *but also essential for teacher growth.* Trying new things makes us attentive, alive in the moment.

When we taught ninth graders together from across the country, Penny suggested that we connect our classes by having our students create and exchange "Where I'm From" digital compositions (based on the George Ella Lyon poem). This meant we each needed to create a model for our students to see. This was no problem for Penny, who was already well versed in creating short digital films. For Kelly, however, whose digital skills were—to put it kindly—a bit behind the curve, this created uneasiness.

Before heading into the classroom, Kelly arranged a tutoring session with Penny. She taught him some of the introductory skills, but it was so new to Kelly, he still did not feel anywhere near prepared a few days later as he began the unit with his students. It was at that point that Kelly made a scary decision: instead of standing in front of his students and pretending to be the expert, he identified students who had advanced skills in digital composition and asked them to take leadership roles. If you want to learn how to create an iMovie, meet in this pod with Kristina. If you are interested in learning how to do voice-overs in a Google slideshow, meet over here in Sennie's group. And so on. Once the groups were set up, Kelly joined one so he could sit in and learn alongside his students. Truthfully, he wasn't sure at the time that this was the right move—it was scary to relinquish his authority—but looking back, he loves how this played out in his classroom. A spirit of student-led collaboration emerged. Students taught students, and when Kelly got stuck, students taught him.

This experience taught Kelly that the best way to get over his fear was to confront it head-on. Since we are certain the digital world will continue to expand—and since this will remain a critical literacy for our students—we recognize that avoiding this reality will only make it worse. We must overcome the fear factor. The sooner, the better.

In Chapter 3, we shared the insights we gained from creating our own poetry as well as some thinking about the implications this creative process had on teaching a poetry study. Here, we repeat this process through the lens of digital composition. In Figure 4–1 you will find the insights we gained from creating our own digital compositions, along with the implications this creative process had on our teaching.

Belief 4: It's time for a trade

Growing up, Kelly was a fan of the California Angels, and for many years his favorite player was their all-star shortstop, Jim Fregosi. When Kelly was ten, he actually met his idol (at the grand opening of a supermarket, of all things) and got an autographed baseball, which sat for years on a shelf above his bed. Life was beautiful, until one day when the unthinkable happened: the Angels traded their aging shortstop! Talk about a loss of innocence! How could they do such a thing? Worse, the Angels had the gall—the temerity—to trade him for a pitcher Kelly had never heard of: some young guy by the name of Nolan Ryan. Kelly was crushed.

Crushed, that is, until Nolan Ryan showed up in Anaheim and started striking everyone out. While Fregosi's career flamed out with the Mets, Ryan went on to become the greatest pitcher in Angels' history, earning multiple all-star selections while throwing four no-hitters in his eight-year tenure. As painful as it was when it happened, this turned out to be the greatest trade in Angels' history.

It is now time for a curriculum trade—one we know you might find painful. We are reminded of our colleague who insisted on teaching his favorite book, *A Separate Peace*, every year, even though kids didn't read it. This was malpractice, frankly; what is best for the teacher

Insight	Implication(s) for Teaching
Learning is incremental.	You do not learn how to make a short film in one swoop. There was a point in the process where Kelly learned how to drop photos in, but he still didn't know how to align the music. He had to practice one skill before learning the next. He also had to let his uneasiness about not understanding all of the parts sit there while he worked on the parts he could understand. We must encourage students to embrace a building-block approach.
Students know more than we do.	We are confident that by the time you read this, our students will have already moved on to newly invented digital apps. This means we may never feel fully qualified to teach digital composition. We must continue to learn from students, which is not a bad place for a teacher to be. One caveat: Although some students will be savvier than the teacher, we should remember that other students will be lost. We must be particularly mindful of students who are behind the technological curve or who may feel ostracized for not having access to technology. They will need additional support.
Collaboration helped us overcome the fear factor.	There were times when we forgot how to do something we had learned. The skill was so new that it didn't stick. We had to go back and ask for help—learn it again—before we could move forward. Additionally, the software continues to evolve, but we don't necessarily know how to use the new versions, so we have to learn again. Being able to sit next to someone who knows the skill is essential for our sustained engagement with this hard work. Teachers should consider allowing students to create collaboratively, as they will offer expertise and comfort to one another.
Find joy in the creative process.	Collecting photos for our films was fun. We lost track of time rifling through the possibilities. We found new photos and deleted others, and the idea that this project was gradually getting better fueled our commitment. Even though Kelly's final product wasn't as polished as Penny's, he was proud of his progress. He didn't want to compare it with others' work, but he could see that he had come a long way composing with digital tools. He learned a lot, and that felt good. When we find joy in our process, we have to make that visible to our students.
Consider next steps.	Self-reflection after the creation is critical. Kelly, for example, learned how to sequence his images, how to overlap a soundtrack, and how to animate captions on the screen. But when he compared his movie with others, he identified areas he could learn to do better next time. His transitions are rough, his pacing is too slow, and he'd like to add his own voice-over. We want students to consider key questions: What can I do now that I couldn't do before? What do I want to learn next? To whom can I turn to help me learn this?

Figure 4–1 Insights from Composing Digital Compositions

is not always best for the students. "This is something I love to teach!" is not the same thing as "This is something my students really need." We recall the words of the writer Jason Reynolds, who, in looking back on his disengagement in high school English classes, wanted to say to his teachers, "You traded *my* engagement for books *you* cared about" (2020).

Let us never forget that curriculum *must evolve.* To build and maintain student engagement, our teaching needs to be responsive to the children in the room. In a digital world, we cannot imagine teaching an entire year without addressing one of today's critical literacies. Yes, it may be hard to let go of a unit you have taught for years, but our students have changed. So have their interests and needs. This means we need to change as well.

So, go ahead. Make the trade.

Belief 5: The process of composing is more important than the product

It's the process, not the product. It's a little perplexing that this statement has to be resaid sixty years after Donald Murray published it in a series of essays for *College English*. Murray changed the landscape of writing instruction by asking this question of himself and his colleagues: *Why don't we teach young writers how writers work?* As a practicing journalist, he learned to draft and revise and ask for feedback. Why didn't teachers put more emphasis on those habits?

Murray noted that the primary curriculum at the University of New Hampshire had students read a collection of published essays and write about them. Professors marked them up with corrections and graded them. Murray questioned the teachers' inclination to assign topics and grade them, week after week. It wasn't that teachers didn't value the process; they didn't know how to teach it because they didn't write themselves. This is, unfortunately, still true in many classrooms.

Don Graves expanded on Murray's thinking:

> The teaching of writing demands the control of two crafts, teaching and writing. They can neither be avoided, nor separated. The writer who knows the craft of writing can't walk into a room and work with students unless there is some understanding of the craft of teaching. Neither can teachers who have not wrestled with writing, effectively teach the writer's craft. We don't find many teachers of oil painting, piano, ceramics, or drama who are not practitioners in their fields. Their students see them in action in the studio. They can't teach without showing what they mean. There is a process to follow. There is a process to learn. That's the way it is with a craft, whether it be teaching or writing. There is a road, a journey to travel, and there is someone to travel with us, someone who has already made the trip. (1983, 180)

This digital literacies study requires the teacher to shift the gaze from what students produce to how those students revise, rethink, reorder, and learn to make small improvements in their work. For this reason, it might be the perfect place to begin to shift your practice as a teacher if you are new to the profession or to the teaching of writing. (There is no shame in recognizing where you start from and making small, incremental steps to improve. In fact, Tom Newkirk talks about the value in trying to get 5 percent better each year. This means you'll be exponentially better in ten years.) You can let go of making a perfect digital project. Don't sweat the criteria; instead, focus on learning from your students. Jump into the possibilities of this study and set up ways to observe and understand your students better. How do they work? What hangs them up? What systems and structures support them and which block their progress? Consider this as a way to study your classroom as a workshop.

One thing we've learned is that the practice of revision increases because the work itself is engaging. Students rewatch their movies and listen to their recordings again and again, considering how a viewer will see and understand their work. This practice happens as they create, and it can involve hours of work. Joe wrote in his endnotes on a project for Penny's class, "I made sure to keep rewatching the movie just so I could see if the viewer could follow my thought process easily." We want students to practice how revising improves their focus and effectiveness. The process they learn transfers across genre.

Belief 6: Collaboration is essential in deepening an understanding of digital composition

Years ago, a groundbreaking study, *Writing Next*, found eleven elements of effective writing instruction proven to elevate the writing abilities of fourth- to twelfth-grade students (Graham and Perin 2007). One of the recommendations is that students should work collaboratively to plan, draft, revise, and edit their compositions. Having students compose together showed "a strong impact on improving the quality of students' writing" (16). *Writing Next* was referring to written compositions, but we have found the same principle holds true when it comes to asking our students to create digital compositions. Creating partnerships has a strong impact on improving of our students' digital composition skills.

To promote collaboration, and to help students start to think about the decisions that go into creating digital compositions, we share an advertisement with them (see Figure 4–2).

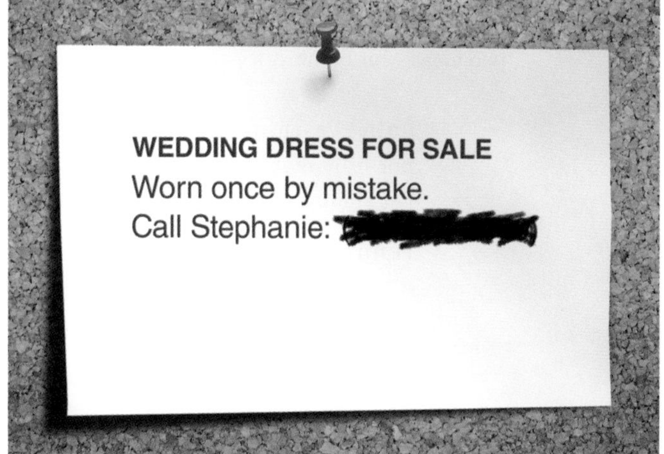

Figure 4–2 Wedding Dress Advertisement

We ask students to imagine how this ad might be turned into a short film. They will not be creating the film; they will simply talk through the decisions that they'd need to make if they were to do so. For example, we might ask, "What would be your opening image? Share thinking with a partner." This leads to animated discussion:

> "We should open the film at the altar!"
>
> "No, we should film her crying as she takes the dress out of the back of her closet."
>
> "Maybe we should start with someone calling her to buy the dress."

After they share possible opening scenes, we then ask, "What music would you select to accompany these scenes?" We continue this probing, asking them to consider other elements of filmmaking (e.g., "Whom would you cast? What locations would you use?").

This is a preview of the spirit of collaboration that will be needed in the study going forward. We believe collaborative composition is important, and this genre is an ideal fit for it.

Belief 7: Digital composition expands multigenre thinking

Penny sits next to Sully to see what he is planning for his final project in ninth-grade English. Sully tells her that his initial plan was to make a video version of his favorite childhood book, *The Little Engine That Could*, but he has decided he doesn't have enough time to make it. Instead, seeking new inspiration, he looked through his notebook, landing on a fictional piece he wrote about a bomb that went off in a city, where "there was carnage all around." Sully tells Penny that rereading this piece reminded him of 9/11 and that it spurred him to go online to watch news reports about that fateful day. Now, sitting in this conference, he wonders if he might meld these two ideas—his bomb story and the news events of 9/11—into one project:

> **Sully:** I'm thinking of doing, like, a short story about it—and kind of possibly maybe do a multinarrator—and I was wondering if I could get some advice on how to tie in the news reports.
>
> **Penny:** I love what you just did. One is that you have had some vision already and you have a really specific question you are asking me. And the other is . . . you are actually going to take something you know is well written, but you are going to do something else with it. I think that is really interesting thinking.
>
> **Sully** (*Begins to consider how this melding might work*): So I might describe something and then I'll go to a like a news report where it

has some people talking about . . . or describing how it was. And so it is all relating to the same thing and kind of adding to it.

Penny (*Affirms his thinking and then encourages Sully to revisit his idea of a multinarrator approach*): Wouldn't it be interesting to bring the character in your story to the scene? Or a police officer or firefighter? (*This line of questioning inspires Sully.*)

Sully: I was kind of thinking maybe I could do something with a movie or a podcast because I like that kind of stuff. So maybe I write this whole thing and then I record it as a podcast and then I put in the news reports as a video . . .

Penny: Oh, I like that . . . so . . . the entire piece would become a podcast?

Sully: And I might, put in, maybe, like, still shots of newspaper front pages . . .

Penny: How would you do that in a podcast?

Sully: Well, no, I would do it in an iMovie.

After more than seventy combined years in the classroom, we are fluent in speaking Teenager, so allow us to translate part of this conference. When Sully began by saying, "I don't have time to make a movie," he really meant "I am not invested in my first idea; therefore, I am going to dial down my effort." It is interesting, however, that Sully left the conference four minutes later in a completely different mindset—he had a new idea to make a movie.

So what changed his mind? What was the recipe that sparked Sully's newfound enthusiasm? Start with the central ingredient: choice. Mix in a heavy dose of freedom to create. Fold in a subtle nudge or two from his teacher—and in a four-minute span, Sully went from making a film of a children's book, to creating a multinarrator story, to considering the creation of a podcast, before finally deciding on making a movie about 9/11 that blended stories with news accounts.

Sully's journey again highlights the notion that we do not want our young writers to be hamstrung by the Common Core's strict (and false) notion that all writing falls within one of three very narrow lanes: narrative, informational text, and argument. Digital composition—much like the essay writing we discuss in Chapter 1—encourages students to break free from these straightjackets. We give them room to be creative, to blend genres. This is a refreshing departure for students like Sully, whose notion of school writing had been largely defined by teachers, as he yawned through one literary analysis essay after another. Sully's enthusiasm for his project was fueled by his desire to mix stories with information.

Practices Most Important in Teaching Digital Composition

We have four essential practices for teaching digital composition: designing a four-week study for this work; using targeted minilessons in four ways; helping students uncover the potential misinformation or manipulation in digital compositions; and allowing for lots of feedback throughout the study.

Practice 1: We plan a four-week study

The monthlong digital composition study is divided into two stages: creating minidocumentaries and creating a project of the student's choice.

Stage 1: Cocreating a minidocumentary (one week)

We ask students to create minidocumentaries that lift up someone in the community. Students can select a friend, a neighbor, a teacher, a coach, a grandmother—anyone they feel is worthy of highlighting in a one- to two-minute film. They will use photographs, text, music, and video to capture the person. We show them student-made films from previous years (e.g., a profile on a sister who worked in an assisted living facility and a close-up on Laurel Smith, a local Olympic skier).

Students create these films in pairs, and they have one week of class time to complete them. Our goal during this week is to analyze what they know, where they are, and what they need to know. We are up and constantly working the room, dropping in to gauge their concerns and progress. On the board, we keep an anchor chart of the skills we notice emerging, alongside the names of expert students who have mastered these skills: "If you need to know how to create captions, go see Michael, Sandra, or Olivia" or "If you want help on how to align your music, go visit Nadeen or Adele." We want the classroom to become a workshop, and to alleviate student anxiety, we do not grade this first attempt at filmmaking. We simply give credit or no credit. This stage is about unpressured practice and collaboration.

At the end of the week we exchange films between our classes. This not only enables our students to "travel" outside of their cultural bubbles but also allows them to see some of the moves young filmmakers make in the other class. The more mentor texts they see, the more they may adopt new ideas when heading into the second stage of the unit.

Stage 2: Creating a self-selected project (three weeks)

We invite you to create a workshop that frees students to select one digital literacy to learn well. Not all of them, just one. Your students will not all produce the same thing. While one student works on a podcast, another will work in a moviemaking program to tell a story, and another may write an original song and produce a music video. This vision of students working in concert, but each playing their own instrument, is anchored by the research of our mentors Don Graves, Donald Murray, Nancie Atwell, Linda Rief, and Tom Romano.

So why not have all students create the same thing? Having exposure to students working in many mediums makes us all stronger. The media we consume is continually expanding. If we aimed this unit at only one digital literacy (moviemaking, for example), we wouldn't have time to study others. And what if our focus missed the mark? What if we built a unit around movies and the constantly creative world we live in revealed something else entirely by the time this book was published a few months later? Who knew how popular podcasts would become? Who knew how TikTok would explode across the world?

We teach a process.

As new digital literacies are revealed, we want students who can imagine creating in those genres. So what is the task? We ask each student to focus on getting better at one of several visual or audio compositions. Following are some of the visual (movie) composition options.

Create a movie from a notebook entry: We ask students to reread their notebooks in search of something they've written (a poem, a list, a description, a portrait, a bit of story, a letter, an argument) that they can imagine as a film.

Design a public service announcement (PSA): Students create a one-minute commercial designed to persuade an audience to take a favorable action. For inspiration, we encourage them to look at numerous examples found on YouTube. We collect student samples as well from prior years.

Capture a year: Students capture the importance of a specific year. We start them with Chuck Braverman's (1969) "1968" (available on YouTube) as a mentor text, because it contains only two variables, photographs and music. Students can select years that connect to them personally (e.g., the year they were born; their senior year in high school), or they can choose a year of historical significance (e.g., 2020, the year of a global pandemic). Penny modeled the creation of this form in her class as she tried to capture the first year of her granddaughter Maisie's life. Kelly's model centered on the year he graduated from high school.

Capture a day in the life: Students create a snapshot portrait of one day in the life of someone they are curious about: a high school student, their dog, or a fast-food worker. Students have created movies of preparing for a day of ski racing and of setting up a food truck in a local park. This two- to three-minute project is built on curiosity.

Argue a position: We begin by having the class analyze "You Can Do This, Donald Trump," by Chai Dingari of the *New York Times* (2020). We have all students watch it once, then we turn off the sound and encourage them to share observations with each other as we play it again. We urge them to consider several questions: How does the narrator's voice add to the text? What do you notice about the sequencing? What do you notice about the placement of text on the screen? Why that font? Why that size? How would you describe the tone of the piece? Why did the author choose so many young children as examples?

Make a book trailer: Penny's ninth graders created book trailers one spring. The most memorable project was made by a group of boys who summarized the plot of *Percy Jackson and the Olympians: The Lightning Thief* by acting it out. They analyzed dozens of student-made trailers as well as professionally produced movie trailers to deepen their thinking in this genre.

Design a music video: We ask our students, "What is the story you see when you hear a favorite song? Can you capture that?" Through YouTube, we share examples like OneRepublic's "I Lived" (Jones 2014), which combines storytelling and interviews to show the intention of the lyrics. Or One Direction's "Story of My Life" (Mandler 2013), which overlays photographs of the band members' lives over the years. Some of Penny's students have mimicked Taylor Swift's "22" (Winston 2013) by holding stacks of books and singing, "I'm reading twenty-two" (instead of singing, "I'm feeling twenty-two"). Bringing their visions to life is a lot of work, but the creation is energizing. We encourage students who select this project to map out their thinking via storyboards, as this has proven to help them manage the parts.

If students don't want to make a video, we offer several choices for audio compositions. We first used voice recordings in our teaching to hear how all of our students read aloud without scheduling additional one-on-one conferences. We were aware that some students would feel self-conscious reading aloud in front of peers, but we also knew a read-aloud would give us a window into students who struggled with reading. We asked students to record a passage from their independent reading books.

We gave them just three criteria for the assignment:

1. Read this the way you think the author envisioned you hearing it.
2. Read with a slow enough pace so a listener who doesn't know the story (me) can understand the passage.
3. Work to make each word and sentence clear.

After listening to these initial recordings, we added a fourth criterion, vary the volume, to remind students that monotone is deadly. We used these criteria to emphasize what matters in an effective read-aloud, not for grading. In fact, we did not grade this assignment for years; we simply listened to the recordings while grading other student work after school. We discovered both exceptional performances and students who stumbled over every word. We shared recordings with the reading specialist and helped a few students access services because of this assignment. We wondered how many secondary students had slipped by her before we implemented this practice.

Student recordings (with permission) became interesting book talks we kept on Flipgrid, which spurred students to polish their performances. There was freedom with this project that encouraged expressive, rich readings. And yes, there were students who resisted the assignment, but the assurance that no one would hear it but their teacher encouraged students to record. We emphasized the lifelong usefulness of the skill of reading aloud, reminding them of the critical importance of reading to their own children in the future.

The power of these recordings led us to other uses of this medium, like the following:

Perform two-voice poems: Students select a published poem or an original composition. We encourage students to take a favorite poem and reimagine it for several voices. Students must decide who will read each of the lines and which lines they will read in concert. Students collaborate on how to deliver the lines and how to vary the expressiveness, pace, volume, and clarity of their reading to communicate their understanding more completely.

We introduce all students to this practice by having them select a poem and play with these variables for one class period, ending with a round of voluntary performances.

Make a podcast: According to Statista, 55 percent of Americans have listened to a podcast, and with Spotify's recent $400 million acquisition of *The Ringer*, by Bill Simmons, and *The Joe Rogan Experience*, by Joe Rogan, this is not a medium that will cease to be relevant moving forward (Richter 2020). The growth in podcasting is steady worldwide. Podcasts argue, debate, tell stories, inform, and celebrate curiosities.

We curate a long list of possible mentor texts, including the power of investigative journalism, like *Serial*, by Sarah Koenig, and interview formats, like *Conan O'Brien Needs a Friend*, by Conan O'Brien. For conversations about race, identity, and politics, try *Into the Thick*, by Maria Hinojosa and Julio Ricardo Varela. There are recaps and discussions of favorite shows, like *Office Ladies*, by Jenna Fischer and Angela Kinsey, and *The Hamilcast*, by Gillian Pensavale. Students can imagine a wide range of possibilities in audio form. We love the discussions with authors on *Between the Covers*, by David Naimon. Students will likely discover many more.

In Penny's class partners created podcasts to discuss their Matt de la Peña book club books and then shared them with others in class. These podcasts worked like book talks to encourage students to read another book by the same author.

Do a TED talk: The focus of a powerful TED talk is the audio performance and the passion of the presenter. TED talks can include a few slides, but students must study and imitate how speakers hook an audience, build momentum, establish pace, articulate big ideas, and speak with expression. Minilessons include watching the first fifteen seconds of ten TED talks to discuss what happens in those first moments that either captures their interest or bores them. One former student, for example, began her TED talk seated in the audience and then sang until she reached the stage. The subject of her TED talk was what it takes to become a recording artist.

We sometimes do this project with an entire class, beginning with a series of small steps that are essential in building confidence. We are helping students make the move from PowerPoint presentations where they read off their slides and rarely make eye contact or even face the audience to a live performance in the school auditorium. Students prepare by participating in four short rounds in front of their peers: In one-minute talks, students begin by pitching the subjects of their TED talks, but no note cards are allowed. We (both students and teacher) give each student descriptive feedback on their speaking and ask questions about the subject to encourage further research. Their second performance is two minutes long. Students learn how to pace themselves. The two-minute TED talk may include only two slides with very little text. The third performance, five minutes in length, is the trickiest. Students find they have so much to say and so little time, but they also feel how long five minutes is with everyone watching. All students are working toward a ten-minute TED talk with not more than ten slides. Some students bring props (one wheeled a piano onstage; another used a table with the evolution of mobile phones exhibited across ten years). They first share ten-minute presentations with a group of four students, who give them detailed feedback. We wander and listen in at each group to offer encouragement and suggestions. The final performance is before an audience of hundreds. We invite teachers, students, parents, and community members. No students use notecards during any of the performances. Many report this was the most difficult work of their senior year, but it was the project that made them most proud.

Write an original song and record it: We didn't think of this. Students asked if we would allow this in place of our other suggestions. Some wrote a song and recorded themselves or other voices singing it. Others partnered with musicians to create layered compositions. Students have directed the choral group from their church or high school to perform their song. One duo created a song for the school musical. Another student won the schoolwide talent show with the rap he'd written and practiced in class for this study.

Structuring the study

So how do we organize our classrooms to support such variation? There are several good project-based books, notably *Writing Outside Your Comfort Zone: Helping Students Navigate Unfamiliar Genres*, by Cathy Fleischer and Sarah Andrew-Vaughn (2009), and *Project-Based Writing: Teaching Writers to Manage Time and Clarify Purpose*, by Liz Prather (2017). We have learned from them. We have borrowed their good ideas to create structures that support both students and teachers in this process.

Our structures and routines are the guardrails that keep our students productive as they progress through their projects. Here are some we rely on.

Status checks: We conduct daily status-of-the-class checks. In a quick roll call, we ask each student what they will be working on that day. We keep track of student progress on clipboards. This helps us to determine which students we must get to during conferring time.

Conferences: We confer with some students every day. These conferences are essential. We learn what students need and listen to their questions, concerns, and moments of clarity. We take good notes. We use patterns in a class to determine our next minilessons or when we need to gather a small group to learn together.

Student experts: We create opportunities for students to be teachers. They know skills we do not. When we discover this, we invite others to sign up to learn from those students.

Reflections: Students keep a weekly reflection on their progress (both inside and outside of class) in their writing notebooks. We suggest gathering students during the last five minutes of class to write this entry ("This week I worked on . . ."). As we wander the class, we often informally check in with students by looking at their reflections.

Bibliographies: Students create an annotated bibliography of the mentor texts they study. In five to ten sentences, they explain what each text does well and what they learned. This collection of texts should show a range in the genre. (In a list of podcasts, for example, the student should clarify the difference between investigative journalism and storytelling, interview podcasts, and news or commentary).

Checklists: We provide students with a checklist for project requirements. They keep the checklist in their notebooks and update it regularly. This list is created in class, and it reminds students of the minilessons, the practice, and the elements of digital work that we are studying: On Monday we analyzed a commercial for sound elements. On Tuesday we studied the transitions in a podcast. On Wednesday their rough draft was due. And so on. And even though we teach a digital composition unit each year, the list constantly changes as we find new examples to share and as we discover different ways to improve the clarity of our teaching. We find that it is good for students to have deadlines, and the checklist helps students who are absent to get back on track.

Feedback: When a student shares a project in their writing group, listeners write feedback on two sticky notes ("What I noticed" and "What I wonder") and deliver these notes to the creator of the project. The creator places these notes in their writing notebook. Beyond the writing groups in class, we also encourage each student to receive feedback from an "interested adult," an idea we learned in Cathy Fleischer and Sarah Andrew-Vaughan's *Writing Outside Your Comfort Zone* (2009).

Self-reflection: Students self-reflect on the process at the end of the study. We have students reflect not only on how the finished project met the criteria but also on what they learned in having the freedom to create projects of their choice. (We say more about this in the "Assessment and Grading" section later in this chapter.)

Practice 2: We use minilessons for four distinct purposes

Throughout Penny's years of teaching elementary school and into her eighth-grade classroom, students wrote in any genre all year and she conferred with individuals and small groups to keep them moving forward. As class sizes increased, she moved to genre units of study in an attempt to make her teaching more efficient. It wasn't always. Even a march through lessons in a genre can't keep all students in the same place. See, that's the dilemma for all of us. We know that our students are in different places in their drafting of arguments, but we teach the minilesson on introductions anyway. For some, it is the right lesson at the right time; for others, they haven't even settled on a topic, so the lesson is not yet useful to them. We know writers need time to work out problems and learn from their trials and errors, but we try to march them all at the same pace. We seem to be afraid to move beyond this, even though we know this creates anxiety in writers who find themselves in different places.

For this reason, we try to limit whole-class minilessons, but in this unit we also recognize that there are times when whole-class minilessons are valuable because all students will be able to apply what they learn across all types of digital projects. Figure 4–3 lists a couple of examples of minilessons that benefit all students, regardless of the projects they have selected.

Minilesson for All	How Students Apply the Minilesson Across Digital Projects
All students analyze effective composition moves in a documentary. Students focus on different elements in the digital text that correspond to what they need to learn for their digital texts.	A student who wants to make a movie might study the opening fifteen seconds of the documentary for the way the images precede the title slide. A student who wants to create a podcast studies the opening fifteen seconds of the documentary, paying close attention to how the voices of a sports reporter and the narrator sync together. This helps the student see how using several voices in the opening increases interest in what is to come. And yet another student might watch the same fifteen seconds and pick up a move we had not even thought of.
Study a television commercial to focus just on the transitions. Commercials often move between video and narration and sometimes use music to open or close the commercial.	Students study the tools of transitions for their particular texts. For example, they may notice how the music fades out and the commercial ends with a voice-over. They then consider how this move might be used in a podcast, book trailer, or PSA.

Figure 4–3 Examples of Whole-Class Minilessons

We want our whole-class minilessons to benefit as many students as possible. With this in mind, we design them around four key purposes.

Purpose 1: Increase analysis of digital texts

Analyzing digital texts will help students to understand craft moves across media. They will not leave this unit with a complex understanding of all of those craft moves, however. What each student learns will be different (e.g., Shivani will understand the construction of commercials in a new way, and Jared will know how to maximize the power of his recorded voice). Their creations will lead to deeper learning.

We start with the study of a commercial. The first time they watch it, they write a list of the composition moves they saw in the text. We play the commercial again, this time with the sound off, and students share what they noticed in small groups. We start a class list of craft moves. Students analyze the decisions made: Who is the intended audience? How is music used to set the mood? What images were selected, and why were they selected? How is the voice-over layered in? What words are used? How is the pace established? Does it shift? What is said in the commercial? What is not said?

From the deep study of this commercial, we move on to study a different digital text each day (e.g., an excerpt from a podcast, a clip of a TED talk). These are microlessons of about ten minutes that follow this same design. We teach students to be critical of what they notice, and this helps them to learn elements of the craft to *use* when they get to work on their own. We encourage them to find interesting texts to share with the class. Jon brought in a PSA on hunting; Jeff shared the "best commercial *ever*!" We want students to select their own mentor texts and to be able to articulate how these models helped them.

This is important work. If students do not learn to analyze how digital texts are crafted, they run the risk of mindlessly consuming media designed to manipulate them.

Purpose 2: Help students make organizational decisions

Kelly found the skill of storyboarding to be particularly important for organizing a digital text. In creating his "Where I'm From" video, for example, he storyboarded the sequence of his film before shooting any footage (see Figures 4–4a–c).

Kelly needed to see the images on paper because he couldn't imagine them in a movie without seeing the parts. He modeled reorganizing his first draft of thinking on his storyboard. He asked, "How would this film be different if I began with the lifeguard tower?"

As with all first drafts, Kelly did not stay true to his original storyboard. As he began creating, he realized he had too much to cover, so instead of focusing on various aspects of his hometown, he zeroed in on its beach life. Just like we do when we model our writing process, Kelly shared his thinking in real time with his students as he planned and rethought his sequencing. We model this decision-making to empower students to reimagine their ideas. His students, in turn, created their own storyboards. In Figure 4–5, you will see the initial planning of two ninth graders, Angelica and Andrea, as they began thinking through their cocreated "Where I'm From" project.

Once they've created their storyboards, we introduce a move we saw in Linda Rief's classroom where she has students verbalize their storyboards to peers. The listeners give feedback as to what strikes them as essential and what feels nonessential. Students are encouraged to delete scenes that slow the pace, revising their work *before* drafting. This was especially important for multilingual students.

Another way to think about sequence is to model how we plan to overlay the music. Kelly's first scene is a short video of cruising down the Pacific Coast Highway as he drives under the "Welcome to Huntington Beach" overpass sign. Kelly decided to play the Eagles' "Hotel California" to accompany this scene, but this decision required him to make others. Should the music start before the first image? Or should he wait until the movie started rolling? How much of the song should he play? Where should the song fade and his narration begin?

Purpose 3: Teach skills

We begin by handing students a checklist of digital skills (see Figure 4–6). We ask them to select the skills they already know and use. Are there skills we neglected to include? We use these

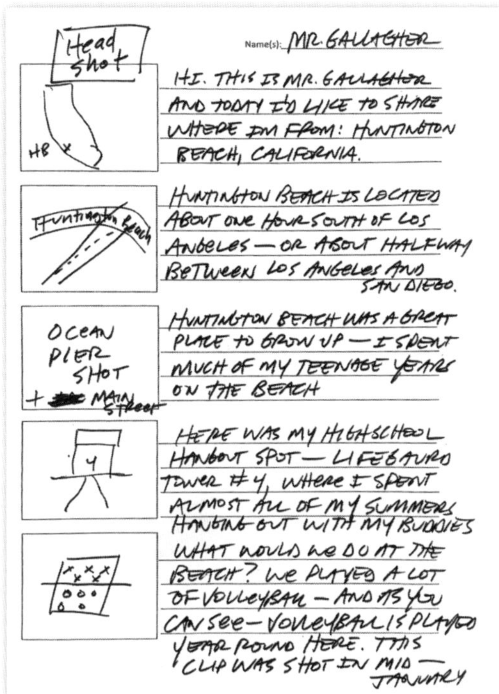

a

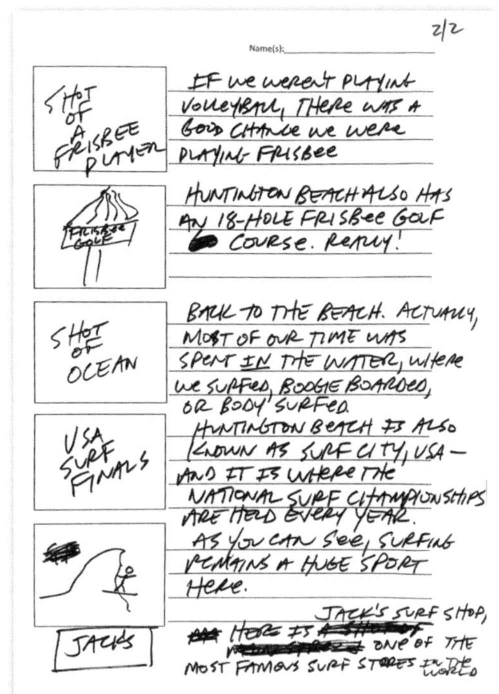

b

c

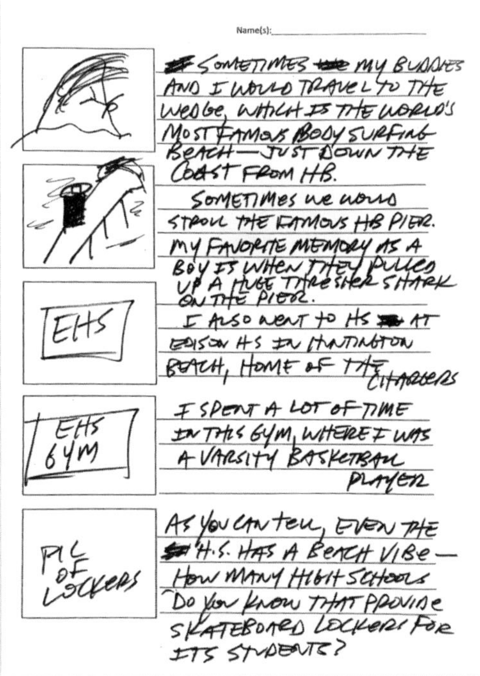

Figure 4a–4c
Kelly's Storyboard

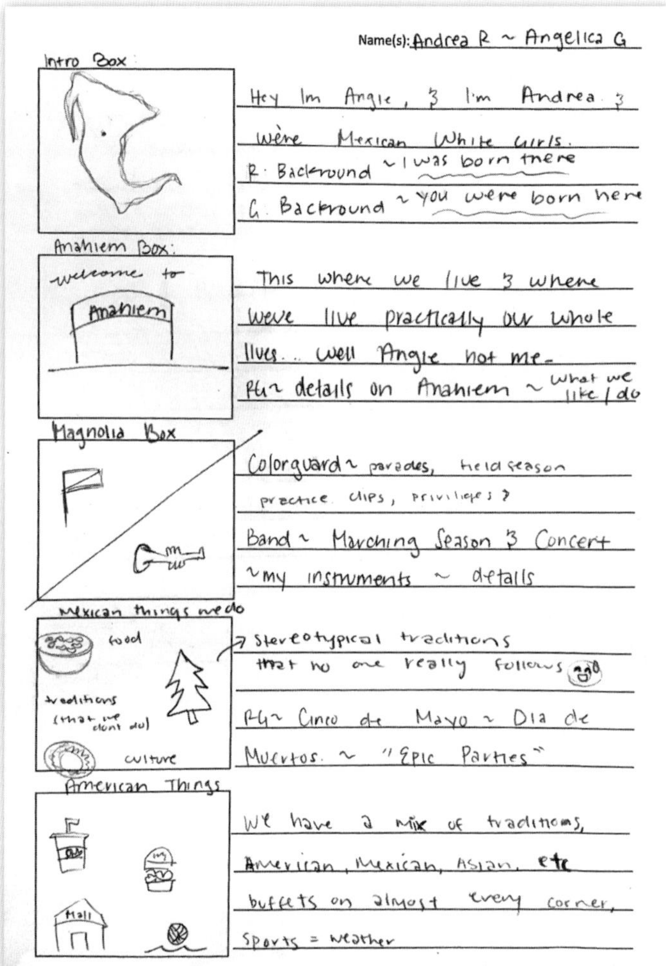
Name(s): Andrea R ~ Angelica G

Intro Box:
Hey Im Angie, & I'm Andrea &
we're Mexican White girls.
R. Backround ~ I was born there
G. Backround ~ you were born here

Anahiem Box:
welcome to Anahiem
This where we live & where
weve live practically our whole
lives.. well Angie not me.
R&G ~ details on Anahiem ~ what we like / do

Magnolia Box
Colorguard ~ parades, field season
practice clips, privileges &
Band ~ Marching Season & Concert
~ my instruments ~ details

Mexican things we do
food
traditions (that we dont do)
culture
→ Stereotypical traditions
that no one really follows
R&G ~ Cinco de Mayo ~ Dia de
Muertos. ~ "Epic Parties"

American Things
Mall
We have a mix of traditions,
American, Mexican, Asian, etc
buffets on almost every corner,
Sports = weather

Figure 4–5 Angelica and Andrea's Storyboard

checklists to plan brief and specific minilessons: This is how to insert music. This is how to zoom in on a photo. This is how to make a scene fade out. These lessons are followed by extended time for students to practice the skills and to consider how they might infuse them into their projects.

Purpose 4: Share student projects to expand possibilities

As we confer with a student, we might say, "Marcus, I love how your film is progressing. Can we share your progress with the rest of the class?" The class then directs its attention to Marcus' project. Writing groups also meet to share their initial progress. The students watching might think, *There's a move I haven't thought of trying.* When students see another student's project, it enlarges their vision of what's possible.

DIGITAL LITERACY SKILLS

Video Skills

- ☐ Create a title slide.
  - ☐ Use a font that is easy to read.
  - ☐ Include all important information.
- ☐ Insert a photo and focus the reader's attention (zoom in or frame it for your intended purpose).
  - ☐ Adjust lighting or boundaries on a photo for best viewing.
  - ☐ Overlay a title on a photo to provide information for viewers.
- ☐ Use transitions effectively.
  - ☐ Between big ideas and
  - ☐ between scenes in a digital story.
- ☐ Add music to your movie.
  - ☐ Adjust volume to a comfortable listening level.
  - ☐ Reduce volume of music to highlight narration.
- ☐ Add video footage from files or pulled from the internet.
  - ☐ Edit video to remove boring parts and emphasize what is important.
- ☐ Bring your digital project to a close with images, music, quotes, or a voice-over—provide a sense of closure for viewers.
- ☐ Save the movie as a file.
- ☐ Use a file sharing program to elicit peer response.

Podcast Skills

- ☐ Study a variety of podcasts (investigative, informative, interview, commentary, entertainment).
- ☐ Plan your podcast with a storyboard or a time line (e.g., plan questions for an interview and length of response).
- ☐ Record a voice-over with attention to pace, expressiveness, volume, and clarity.
- ☐ Weave voices together in an interview, eliminating dead space.
- ☐ Balance voice-over and sound effects.
- ☐ Use sound effects to set the mood early in the podcast.
  - ☐ Find sound effects online that can be downloaded for free.
  - ☐ Download and create a works cited list.
- ☐ Plan breaks or interludes in your podcast (breathing room for listeners).
- ☐ Use sound to bring closure to your podcast.
- ☐ Save the podcast as a file.
- ☐ Use a file sharing program to elicit peer response.

(continues)

DIGITAL LITERACY SKILLS

Writing Process Skills

- ☐ Study digital projects—don't just watch them; study how they work, looking for techniques you can use in your digital project.
- ☐ Draft a plan for your digital project using a storyboard or time line.
- ☐ Identify the audience for your digital project.
- ☐ Write a two-sentence outline of your project that focuses your big idea.
- ☐ Meet deadlines to share thinking and drafts with your writing group.
    - ☐ Share your digital story with at least two people and record notes on their feedback in your notebook so you won't forget their wise advice.
- ☐ Analyze your digital story like a viewer, examining what is working to plan revisions.
    - ☐ Use feedback from others to revise and improve your movie.
- ☐ Reflect on your process of creating this digital story and consider ways you can improve it for future writing and digital compositions.

Figure 4–6 Checklist of Digital Skills

Practice 3: We help students to see how information can be distorted in digital compositions

We have all seen Geico commercials that claim, "Fifteen minutes could save you 15 percent or more on car insurance," but a critical reader of this text would ask some pointed questions: What does "*could* save" mean? Does that imply "could not" as well? Are these savings universally true across all insurers? Across all drivers? Across all regions? And even if I save, is the coverage comparable? When analyzing digital media, it is important to carefully consider what is *not* said. The creators of short digital texts (e.g., PSAs, campaign ads) almost always present incomplete pictures. They leave stuff out. They manipulate information because they want you to believe in the dangers of tobacco, or why you should buy a Ford truck, or why their candidate deserves your vote.

When creating their own digital compositions, students come to understand that they, too, have to condense the information they gather. When Ashton, for example, decided to create a PSA warning against the health dangers associated with marijuana, she collected research from numerous sources to support her position. But she realized that there was no way to shoehorn all of that research into a sixty-second film. In order to create a project that remained tight and focused, she had to make key editorial decisions. What research should go in? And what research could she leave out?

Ashton learned what creators of digital texts do. They streamline. They cut. They leave things unsaid. Ashton developed a healthy skepticism when consuming other digital media. Because she knows the act of truncating can distort or abbreviate truths, she now recognizes that there is an incompleteness in much of what she consumes. A digital text with a strong voice-over has a sense of certainty—when Morgan Freeman tells you something, you believe it—but it sounds more true than perhaps it is. Having made her own film, she can't help but now wonder what Morgan Freeman has left out.

Practice 4: We believe in the importance of midprocess feedback

Feedback throughout the writing process on any project is important, but we believe it takes on an even greater role in this unit. Digital composition invites procrastination. There's a reason this happen, as Ira Glass says:

> Nobody tells people who are beginners and I really wish somebody had told this to me, is that all of us who do creative work, we get into it because we have good taste. But it's like there is a gap. What you're making isn't so good. . . . It's trying to be good. It has ambition to be good . . . but your taste, the thing that got you into the game, your taste is still killer and your taste is good enough that you can tell that what you're making is kind of a disappointment to you. A lot of people never get past that phase. They quit. (in Liu 2011)

We have seen students stymied simply by the range of options in digital composition. They feel less confident than usual and hesitant to start. Some quit trying. Seeing what other students are making can get these students working.

During the first week we roam the room looking for examples of work we can share with the class. We want to provide students with a vision that is between the polish and professionalism of published work and the blank screen. When we see a movie that is partially done, we ask, "Would you be willing to share this with the class and let them help you think through the challenges you are facing at this stage?" Almost all say yes.

Whole-class midprocess feedback can be a minilesson to launch class. We might also use a teaching move called catch and release: when you notice a lot of students struggling with the same skill, bring the class together to briefly reteach it. This is more efficient than addressing the same content many times in individual conferences.

The process of using student drafts to teach the whole class follows the same structure we practice in writing groups: the author of the piece elicits feedback (e.g., "I'm wondering if my pacing feels right. Is my commercial moving too quickly?"). The writer's request for specific feedback encourages students to watch closely, which leads them to learn techniques and ideas they might try on their own projects. We participate as a member of the class, as we consider how we can use the student's work to inspire others. We create a link between a student who knows a digital composition craft move with those in the room who don't.

We have a first-draft deadline, when students are expected to meet in writing groups to share their movies. Some students will not meet this deadline. But others will. And having our writing groups meet and discuss a few movies is better than letting students continue to flounder. If all students in one group show up empty-handed, we just assign each to a different group for the day.

With a project this complex, we encourage regular feedback throughout the process. We model our struggles and the language of a growth mindset: "My movie feels more complete since I added the photos of my mom's early years. I also changed the music to match the time when the pictures were taken. I can see the growth I'm making and what I need to work on next."

Midprocess feedback is not evaluative (good or bad) but reflective: "I am feeling more confident about this, while I am still struggling with that." The only time we refer to the criteria for the project is to celebrate what the student has done so far or to remind students of something they may have forgotten.

When it comes to midprocess feedback, the more, the better. We were once athletes and know that coaching is more useful during practice and at halftime than once the game is over. We spend more time commenting on drafts while students are working on them than once they are finished.

Assessment and Grading

Assessment

Assessment is an opportunity for students to take stock of where they are and where they need to grow. It allows the teacher to gauge what is going well and where support is needed. It is information gathering. It involves both the teacher and the student. We have outlined a number of assessment practices for both students and teachers already in this chapter:

Student Assessment

- weekly reflections of progress and challenges
- a project checklist to remind students of expectations
- analysis of their project next to a list of criteria

Teacher Assessment

- status-of-the-class checks
- peer response groups where a teacher listens in and keeps notes
- one-on-one conferring
- small groups where students teach skills

We believe these assessments are more important for student growth than evaluation is, but we also recognize that almost all schools require grades.

Excellence in Digital Composition

How can we evaluate their work with integrity? There is no CCSS guidance here. No scope and sequence for practicing digital tools. No commonly produced expectations for grade-level performance. Grading digital compositions grows even more complicated by the reality that some will come to class with advanced skills, while others will be standing at the starting line. This raises equity issues. Some students are from technology-rich homes, while others are not. We've had students shoot videos using their own drones and turn in their projects alongside homeless students who did not even own phones. How do you grade that disparity equitably?

We also worry about the negative effects grades can have on student motivation and performance. Take Kelly's first foray into filmmaking—his "Where I'm From" video highlighting his childhood in Huntington Beach. Kelly's completed video is rough. But he is proud of this video because he entered the project with zero experience, and as rough as it is, Kelly learned a lot. Would it be fair to judge his video next to a rubric that outlines perfection? Would it be fair to compare his video against one made by Penny "Spielberg" Kittle, who has been making films for years? (Inference practice: can you guess which one of us wrote the last sentence?)

When thinking about grading, we must also remember that this study is an outlier. What do we mean by this? Students have been telling stories since they learned to speak. In many classrooms they are allowed to write those stories, both as fiction and nonfiction, throughout their years in school. By the time they get to high school, teachers assume (sometimes wrongly) that students have a body of experience with writing stories, so they align their grading with criteria that they believe all students can reach. This study is different, however. We can't penalize those who have never been taught digital skills before arriving in our classrooms. All grading raises issues of fairness. Because this is a new set of skills, the issue is exacerbated here and leads us to think more deeply about how grading affects students across all genres.

Our uneasiness echoes those of our favorite author on grading and assessment, Maja Wilson: "Variations on this question have plagued my career. When I started teaching over twenty years ago, I tried to avoid assessment. I just wanted to write with my students. Nothing killed the joyfulness of that labor like a grade or score, and I was confident that we'd all improve anyway if we kept writing and talking about our writing" (2021). But alas . . . the gradebook awaits. Judgment day looms. So how might you grade these projects? Consider one of these two grading approaches, both of which we have used in our classrooms.

Approach 1: Provide a clear target

We present students with criteria to aim for, not a rubric (see Figures 4–6, which we discussed earlier, and 4–7). Just because we have provided a target does not mean we are finished with decision-making. Will this be an effort grade because students made an attempt with all of the criteria? Or will this be a skills grade where we evaluate the effective use of each skill? We write comments next to each category (e.g., "Here your pace effectively communicates the urgency of this issue, but here I wonder if you could edit the video to get to the point more quickly?").

When we look at the project as a whole, we give it a holistic grade. We do not add up numbers and divide by five. All skills are not of equal value. One element may be done so skillfully that it deserves more weight than editing a few text slides. We're sure you realize that as soon as we wade into the issue of grading, we uncover how truly complex these decisions are.

Approach 2: Make grading contracts

We begin the unit by having students assess what they know and what they do not know in the creation of digital compositions (see the list of skills in Figure 4–6). Students self-reflect on learning and set goals for what they will learn during this unit. It doesn't matter where they start. What matters is their progress. At the end of the unit, students write about their learning journey, considering these questions:

- How did the focus of your digital composition change as you created it?
- Did your original idea expand or contract?

Digital Composition Project

CATEGORY	EXCELLENCE IN DIGITAL COMPOSITION
Organization	Establishes a clear purpose or big idea and maintains a focus on it throughout the text. Images and video are organized to work together and to best engage a viewer.
Pacing	The pacing of photographs and video fits the idea and maintains audience interest by being neither too fast nor too slow. A varied pace is best. There is just the right amount of detail. The movie does not drag, nor does it speed past important moments.
Images	The images are visually pleasing and communicate the tone of the whole text. Thought went into the focus on images or video in relation to the background of the setting.
Media	There is a combination of photographs and video and recorded voice-overs as well as text slides when needed and music that sets the tone. All audio is adjusted to maintain a comfortable sound level for the audience.
Editing	Spelling and punctuation are correct on text slides. Transitions are creative and do not distract viewers between sections of the video.

COMMENTS on your process or other things I should consider as I review your work:

____

____

____

Figure 4–7 Criteria for Digital Composition

- Explain the revisions you made.
- What feedback was most helpful to you?
- If you had more time to work on this, what would you spend time on?

The teacher reads each student's reflection and then conducts a short grading conference to review progress and learning. The grade is negotiated. We ask the student, "Given the goals you set for yourself at the beginning of the unit, what grade have you earned for this project?" We have found that most students are harder on themselves than we are. They are quick to see their faults and less able to identify their strengths. In the rare case that a student proposes a grade far higher than we expect, we return to the criteria and ask the student to identify when and where they met these expectations. This is a teaching opportunity. We welcome this conversation.

We don't know how much freedom you have to make grading decisions. We don't know your students. We don't know the grading pressures from your department, your administrators, and parents. We do know that grading sends a message. It is one way we communicate with our students. But here's a question we always wrestle with: Do our grades have a positive effect on engagement, curiosity, and confidence?

Closing Thoughts

How many years have we been talking about a digital revolution that would transform education? And yet, so many classrooms have moved only in superficial ways. A student writes an essay on a computer instead of by hand, which, in the words of former president Barack Obama, adds only "a mask of tidiness to half-baked ideas" (2020, xiii). Classrooms remain lecture-centered, only students are now receiving information through PowerPoint presentations. Teachers are still posing questions, but students are now posting their responses on digital bulletin boards. Rather than helping to reimagine curriculum, technology has simply put a shine on the same units that we've been teaching for years.

We must change this.

What if we stopped simply revising last year's units and shifted our gaze forward into the world of our students? What if we were to see emerging technologies as tools to help us redesign our curriculum? To more deeply understand the composition process? What if we took the advice of Jal Mehta, professor in the Harvard Graduate School of Education, who suggests we "discard the many topics that have accumulated like old souvenirs, while retaining essential knowledge and topics that spark joy" (2020)? There's a thought! What if sparking joy became a central goal in our classrooms? Why is this a radical idea?

You might start "discarding old souvenirs" by sitting with colleagues and analyzing your department's current curriculum. You probably will not see digital composition in your scope and sequence, and yet, this is what kids are reading the most outside of class. This realization is an invitation to ask critical questions: *Why are we not teaching digital composition in a digital world? Kids are reading lots of novels and writing lots of essays—could one of these experiences be traded to make room for the creation of digital compositions? Would this new unit result in an increase in student engagement and revision practice both inside and outside of class?*

And while you are in this reflective space, invite your students into these conversations. Ask them: *Is your creativity being honored? Is the curriculum aligned with preparing you for life after high school? What do you need more of? Less of?* We predict their responses will give you motivation to try something new.

Deviating from the standing curriculum will take courage, of course, but we see evidence of this kind of courage spreading across the country. For example, teachers are rethinking what students should be reading. How many whole-class texts in our curriculum are written by white men? Where can we make room for inclusive texts? Which books will reignite a lost passion for reading? Asking these questions is a central part of our evolution as teachers. We have to resist when others who do not know our students have decided what is best for them. We have to stop dancing to someone else's song.

And we'd be remiss if we did not mention another benefit that arises when students create digital compositions: they develop compassion for others. Aurelio shows us what living with undocumented parents means. Christina reveals how hard it is to access treatment for the addiction of a beloved brother. Victoria recounts the life of her auntie, who was lost to COVID-19. Our students have stories only they can tell, and digital composition lifts their stories off the written page. It animates them. When shared, the stories create a connection—a sense of community. And when students share across schools, it humanizes and broadens their worldview, which, in an extremely fractured time, is more important now than ever.

We leave this chapter by introducing our dogs, Julius and Scout (see Figures 4–8 and 4–9). Though they are different in many respects, they share one characteristic: if you throw a ball, they will run and fetch it. Well, to a point. The key is to start with a short distance and work up to longer distances. Throw the ball thirty feet, and they will return it. Then throw the ball fifty feet, and they will return it. Then throw the ball one hundred feet, and they will still return it. But here is the thing: If you *start* by throwing the ball one hundred feet away, they will lie down at your feet and give you the "This is not happening" look. The key is to start small and gradually work toward the longer distance.

Figure 4–8 Julius Kittle

Figure 4–9 Scout Gallagher

For many teachers, we suspect, a unit in digital composition may feel like retrieving a ball that has been thrown too far away. It's way out there. You may be thinking, *This is not happening.* We understand this hesitation, but we encourage you to embrace your discomfort, to work through it. The rewards are great. If you give it a go, don't throw the ball too far. Start small. Ask permission to pilot one idea. Perhaps remove the pressure from your students (and you) by eliminating grading from the equation. Also, don't be too harsh on assessing *your* teaching performance. Grant yourself grace if the unit does not soar the first time you try it. We have found that it takes three to four attempts for a new study to really take hold. Remember this.

The good news is there is no guidance here. This newness—the uncertainty—is what makes this an exciting study. Bringing novelty into the curriculum is what keeps us and our students alert. When we embrace something new—when we take a risk—we send a powerful message about lifelong learning to our students. They continually reward us by showing what is possible when we break from standardization and embrace their creativity.

So go ahead. Throw the ball.

This afterword is inspired by two authors: Amy Krouse Rosenthal (*Encyclopedia of an Ordinary Life* [2008]) and Frederick Joseph (*The Black Friend* [2020]). See **credit** below.

agency Students do not achieve agency unless they are making decisions. Teachers do not achieve agency unless they are making decisions. (See **compliance**; **courage**.)

antiracist All curriculum is political. We need to confront our own biases and analyze our curriculum. The texts we study with students matter. To be antiracist requires work to change the structures that perpetuate white-centered teaching and learning (see **#DisruptTexts**).

avoidance The necessary conversations about learning that we must have with colleagues are easy to avoid. Be "crazy brave," as Joy Harjo (2019) says.

beliefs There are no random acts of teaching. What we do is grounded in what we believe about learning, about students, and about our ability to make reading and writing irresistible.

blank page, the An opportunity for creation, a blank page should be filled with student energy, stories, song lyrics, surprises, art (see **notebook**).

Book Love Foundation A nonprofit organization that provides funds for book clubs and classroom libraries. Consider applying.

compliance Often masquerades as learning but isn't. Not to be confused with engagement.

composition Composing, whether on the page or in a digital medium, is complex, relevant, and invites creative thinking. Students will rethink and revise naturally, as they imitate the creative power of texts they consume each day.

conferring Yes. Daily. The opposite of **hovering**.

courage What is best for kids is not always popular with teachers. Change will often be met with resistance.

create The highest level of thinking on Bloom's taxonomy is the act of creation. So why is analysis the dominant practice in high school English classes?

credit Acknowledgment matters. There is a long history of appropriation of ideas in education. Some teachers even sell others' ideas on websites. This is deeply wrong. It puts a permanent smudge on integrity. We must respect and acknowledge the labor of others. We teach students how to credit others' writing, photographs, music, lines from poems, and video.

curiosity Ask questions of your teaching. When something nags at you, sit with it. Learn from students, colleagues, professional books, conferences. Keep moving.

curriculum What you teach is ultimately your responsibility. Do not cede it to people who do not live in your classroom.

decisions The most important word in this book. Who's making them in the classroom?

#DisruptTexts A creative collaboration between teachers Tricia Ebervia, Lorena Germain, Dr. Kim Parker, and Julia Torres. Follow them. The critical lens they apply to books is vital for all schools.

do Participate in the work you assign. Model your thinking with your students. Reveal your struggles and breakthroughs.

Dons, the Murray and Graves. All writing teachers should know their work. (See also *Toms, the.*)

freedom For students: to choose books, to choose subjects for writing, to choose projects. For teachers: to design curriculum, to revise it as necessary.

grace Something you should grant yourself when you try something new and it doesn't soar.

Hamnet (O'Farrell 2021) **and *Homeland Elegies*** (Akhtar 2020) Two books we read this year with adults in a Zoom book club. It's hard to appreciate the value of book club conversations if you always read alone. There is joy in bouncing off the thinking of others. It builds community.

hope Lies at the heart of education. We believe in the power of teachers to change the heart of a school.

hovering A disease. It must be treated. A teacher paces the room, checking on everyone, instead of sitting beside a student to have a conversation (see **conferring**).

identity Students must see themselves in what they read and write (see **#DisruptTexts**).

imitation A powerful first step toward creation.

independence Will students read and write on their own? Can they organize or revise without templates and our intervention?

inspiration A contagious force in a classroom (see **do**).

joy We return to things that bring us joy, which leads to deep, lasting learning. We find the time. Every student deserves a book they cannot stop reading and a voice on the page they recognize as their own. Even in high school. Especially in high school.

laughter If you choose a coauthor wisely, laughter will fill a two-year process of writing a book together. We are grateful that the world of teaching brought us together. Most days.

listen When a student feels they are heard and acknowledged, trust develops (see **conferring**).

love 1. Love your students, every one of them. Remind yourself: the least lovable kid is probably the one who most needs you. 2. Love your profession: love books, writing, struggling to make words convey meaning, placing a pen on a blank page in a notebook, revising that thinking, learning from a professional journal or a new book, talking to teachers, learning from poets, attending conferences, listening to student stories, the start of a new year when everything seems possible.

lunch table Sit at the right one. You know what we mean.

midprocess Students need support, not criticism, and they need it while they are in the creative process, not at the finish line.

music playlists We use music to signal it's time to write and help all writers settle into creation.

notebook In a digital age, it is still important for students to write by hand. A notebook is personal, it's portable, and it invites a volume of practice *outside* of class.

novelty	Embrace the power of unexpected things. Repetition can choke curiosity and risk-taking.
#OwnVoices	Who is telling the story? This has enormous implications for shaping our students' understanding of the world. Fill the gaps in your classroom library (see **Book Love Foundation**).
pacing guides	Schedules created by outsiders thwart teacher decision-making. We've all been in a classroom where students have asked, "Can we spend another day on this?" (See **agency**.)
picture books	Like poems, picture books pack big thinking into a small space. They belong in every classroom, regardless of the age of the students.
reflection	The lifeblood of improvement.
rigor	Any project can be rigorous if the work is grounded in active decision-making: how to organize, rethink, rewrite, and struggle with composition.
roots	We need something to anchor us when the ground shifts in education. Our roots reach back decades to writers Louise Rosenblatt and John Dewey and then forward to Cornelius Minor and Bettina Love. The web of many influences deepens and expands our **beliefs**.
rubrics	No. Read Maja Wilson (2006).
rules	We adopt Clint Smith's (2014) four classroom rules: (1) read critically; (2) write consciously; (3) speak clearly; (4) tell your truth.
"standard English"	How we use conventions is dependent on audience and purpose. There is no single standard. "Standard English" in the script of *Hamilton* is different than "standard English" in Tyehimba Jess' Pulitzer Prize–winning collection of poems, *Olio* (2016).
talk	We should talk less so that students talk more.
#TeachLivingPoets	Contemporary poetry connects with contemporary kids. Notebook writing blooms when they practice alongside living poets.
temptations	Templates, order, shortcuts, silence. We avoid messiness in our lives but must embrace it in teaching.
Toms, the	Newkirk and Romano. All teachers should know their work. (See **Dons, the**.)

transform Each year is a living, breathing thing. It should not be a replica of the one before.

ungraded, low stakes Practice is an essential element of a writer's growth. A student's notebook is a place to take risks, to try new moves, to write without fear.

unprepared The number of college students who must enroll in remedial English courses is alarming: They are unable to keep pace with the volume of reading and writing. This is a call to reevaluate our practices.

volume Students *read more* when in book clubs built with high-interest, relevant titles. Students *write more* when they have control of their subject and form. More matters.

vulnerable Writing and revising in front of students creates intimacy. When we reveal our humanity, students are much more likely to reveal theirs.

willpower We learned from Charles Duhigg's *The Power of Habit* that decision making radically increases energy and focus (2014). Our students proved this daily.

wrestling The struggle to write well makes us (teachers and students) stronger. It's supposed to be hard. That's what makes it meaningful.

you Throughout the writing of this book, *you* were at the heart of our thinking. You at your desk in the early light of dawn, looking across your classroom and wondering, *What is possible today?* Determined. Relentless. Creative. We see you.

WORKS CITED

Academy of American Poets. n.d. "Found Poem." Poets.org. https://poets.org/glossary/found-poem.

Adichie, Chimamanda Ngozi. 2009. "The Danger of a Single Story." TED talk presented at TEDGlobal, Oxford, England, July. TED video, 18:19. https://www.ted.com/talks/chimamanda_ngozi_adichie_the_danger_of_a_single_story.

Akhtar, Ayad. 2020. *Homeland Elegies*. New York: Little, Brown.

Alexander, Kwame. 2019. *The Write Thing: Kwame Alexander Engages Students in Writing Workshop (and You Can Too!)*. Huntington Beach, CA: Shell Education.

Anderson, Sam. 2021. "I Recommend Eating Chips." *The New York Times*, January 13. https://www.nytimes.com/2021/01/13/magazine/i-recommend-eating-chips.html.

Armstrong, Patricia. 2010. "Bloom's Taxonomy." Vanderbilt University Center for Teaching. https://cft.vanderbilt.edu/guides-sub-pages/blooms-taxonomy/.

Atwell, Nancie, and Anne Atwell Merkel. 2016. *The Reading Zone: How to Help Kids Become Passionate, Skilled, Habitual, Critical Readers*. New York: Scholastic.

Barnet, Sylvan. 2018. *A Short Guide to Writing About Art*. New York: Pearson. https://www.studentartguide.com/articles/how-to-analyze-an-artwork.

Bayles, David, and Ted Orland. 2014. *Art & Fear: Observations on the Perils (and Rewards) of Artmaking*. New York: Pearson.

Bennett, Dalton, Sarah Cahlan, Aaron C. Davis, and Joyce Sohyun Lee. 2020. "The Crackdown Before Trump's Photo Op." *The Washington Post*, June 8. https://www.washingtonpost.com/investigations/2020/06/08/timeline-trump-church-photo-op/.

Bishop, Rudine Sims. 1990. "Mirrors, Windows, and Sliding Glass Doors." *Perspectives: Choosing and Using Books for the Classroom*. Vol. 6, No. 3.

Blau, Sheridan. 2003. *The Literature Workshop: Teaching Texts and Their Readers*. Portsmouth, NH: Heinemann.

———. 2019. "The Academic Writing Apprenticeship: Helping Students Become More Engaged Writers and Legitimate Participants in the Intellectual Life of Their Classroom Through the Commentary Project, Grades 6–12" (workshop), University of California Irvine's Writing Project, Dec. 5, Irvine, California.

Bomer, Katherine. 2016. *The Journey Is Everything: Teaching Essays That Students Want to Write for People Who Want to Read Them*. Portsmouth, NH: Heinemann.

Bostley, Scout, and Darius Simpson. 2015. "Lost Voices." TEDx talk presented at TEDxDetroit conference, October 8. YouTube video, 3:49. https://www.youtube.com/watch?v =IQTl3VB3ChQ.

Braverman, Chuck, dir. 1969. *60 Minutes*. Season 1, Episode 8, segment "1968." Aired January 7 on CBS. YouTube video, 5:07. https://www.youtube.com/watch?v=vtz5Emyldwg.

Brown, Jericho. 2012. "Jericho Brown." Interview by *The Kenyon Review*. *The Kenyon Review*, October 2. https://kenyonreview.org/conversation/jericho-brown/.

Buckingham, Marcus. 2019. "Everything You Know About Giving Feedback at Work Could Be Wrong." Interview by Jena McGregor. *Washington Post*, February 2. https://www .washingtonpost.com/business/2019/02/20/everything-you-know-about-giving -feedback-work-could-be-wrong/.

Buckingham, Marcus, and Ashley Goodall. 2019. "The Feedback Fallacy." *Harvard Business Review*, March–April. https://hbr.org/2019/03/the-feedback-fallacy.

Burke, Kenneth. 1968. "Psychology and Form." In *Counter-Statement*. 2nd ed. Berkeley: University of California Press.

Caldwell, Gail. 2020. "Learning How to Love from Afar." *The New York Times*, May 22. https://www.nytimes.com/2020/05/22/well/family/coronavirus-polio-neighbors -community.html.

Cedillo, Christina V. 2018. "What Does It Mean to Move? Race, Disability, and Critical Embodiment Pedagogy." *Composition Forum* 39. http://compositionforum.com/issue /39/to-move.php.

Cherry-Paul, Sonja, and Dana Johansen. 2019. *Breathing New Life into Book Clubs: A Practical Guide for Teachers*. Portsmouth, NH: Heinemann.

Christie, Michael. 2015. "All Parents Are Cowards." *The New York Times*, February 12. https:// opinionator.blogs.nytimes.com/2015/02/12/all-parents-are-cowards/.

Coates, Te-Nehisi. 2014. "The Case for Reparations." *The Atlantic*, June 2014. https://www .theatlantic.com/magazine/archive/2014/06/the-case-for-reparations/361631/.

———. 2017. *Between the World and Me*. New York: Spiegel and Grau.

Collins, Billy. 1988. "Introduction to Poetry by Billy Collins." *The Apple That Astonished Paris*. Fayetteville: University of Arkansas Press. www.poetryfoundation.org/poems/46712 /introduction-to-poetry.

Davis, Lydia. 2019. "Lydia Davis: Ten of My Recommendations for Good Writing Habits." Literary Hub, November 12. https://lithub.com/lydia-davis-ten-of-my-recommendations -for-good-writing-habits/.

de la Peña, Matt. 2013. *The Living*. New York: Ember.

Dingari, Chai. 2020. "You Can Do This, Donald Trump." November 7. *The New York Times* video, 1:41. https://www.nytimes.com/video/opinion/100000007440367/trump-concede-speech.html.

Dowd, Maureen. 2019. "Here Be Mother of Dragons." *The New York Times*, April 6. https://www.nytimes.com/2019/04/06/opinion/sunday/game-of-thrones-emilia-clarke.html.

Duhigg, Charles. 2014. *The Power of Habit: Why We Do What We Do in Life and Business*. New York: Random House Trade Paperbacks.

Elbow, Peter. 2011. "Freewriting." http://blogs.ubc.ca/english112/files/2011/09/text-1-peter-elbow-freewriting.pdf.

———. 2012. *Vernacular Eloquence: What Speech Can Bring to Writing*. New York: Oxford University Press.

Espinosa, Cecelia M., and Laura Ascenzi-Moreno. 2021. *Rooted in Strength: Using Translanguaging to Grow Multilingual Readers and Writers*. New York: Scholastic Professional.

Fleischer, Cathy, and Sarah Andrew-Vaughan. 2009. *Writing Outside Your Comfort Zone: Helping Students Navigate Unfamiliar Genres*. Portsmouth, NH: Heinemann.

Foster, Thomas C. 2018. *How to Read Poetry Like a Professor: A Quippy and Sonorous Guide to Verse*. New York: Harper Perennial.

Freire, Paulo. 1968. *Pedagogy of the Oppressed*. New York: Seabury.

Friedman, Todd. 2020. "After Grading the Regents." *English Journal* 109 (6): 19.

Gallagher, Kelly. 2004. *Deeper Reading: Comprehending Challenging Texts, 4–12*. Portland, ME: Stenhouse.

Gallagher, Kelly, and Penny Kittle. 2018. *180 Days: Two Teachers and the Quest to Engage and Empower Adolescents*. Portsmouth, NH: Heinemann.

———. 2020a. "The Curse of 'Helicopter Teaching.'" *Educational Leadership* 77 (6): 14–19.

———. 2020b. "Day 14 April 2, 2020." April 2. Vimeo video, 39:20. https://vimeo.com/403375291.

Glover, Matt, and Mary Alice Berry. 2012. *Projecting Possibilities for Writers: The How, What and Why of Designing Units of Study, K–5*. Portsmouth, NH: Heinemann.

Glover, Matt, and Ellin Oliver Keene. 2015. *The Teacher You Want to Be: Essays About Children, Learning, and Teaching*. Portsmouth, NH: Heinemann.

Graff, Gerald, and Cathy Birkenstein. 2018. *They Say/I Say: The Moves That Matter in Academic Writing*. 4th ed. New York: W. W. Norton.

Graham, Steve, and Dolores Perin. 2007. *Writing Next: Effective Strategies to Improve Writing of Adolescents in Middle and High Schools—A Report to Carnegie Corporation of New York*. Washington, DC: Alliance for Excellent Education.

Graves, Donald H. 1983. *Writing: Teachers and Children at Work*. Portsmouth, NH: Heinemann.

Gray, Hanna Holborn. 2012. *Searching for Utopia: Universities and Their Histories*. Oakland: University of California Press.

Gupta, Divanshi. 2020. "Impact of the Coronavirus Pandemic on Digital Consumption: A Marketing Perspective." *Your Story*, May 23. https://yourstory.com/2020/05/impact-coronavirus-digital-content-consumption-marketing.

Harjo, Joy. 2019. *Crazy Brave: A Memoir.* New York: W. W. Norton.

Ivey, Gay, and Peter H. Johnston. 2013. "Engagement with Young Adult Literature: Outcomes and Processes." *Reading Research Quarterly* 48 (3): 1–21.

Jackson, Mitchell S. 2020. "Twelve Minutes and a Life." *Runner's World*, June 18. https://www.runnersworld.com/runners-stories/a32883923/ahmaud-arbery-death-running-and-racism/.

Jess, Tyehimba. 2016. *Olio.* Seattle, WA: Wave Books.

Johnston, Peter. 2004. *Choice Words: How Our Language Affects Children's Learning.* Portsmouth, NH: Stenhouse.

Jones, Noble, dir. 2014. "I Lived." Official music video, September 25. YouTube video, 5:39. https://www.youtube.com/watch?v=z0rxydSolwU.

Joseph, Frederick. 2020. *The Black Friend: On Being a Better White Person*. Somerville, MA: Candlewick.

Kaye, Phil. 2018. "Camaro." Butten Poetry. August 12. YouTube video, 3:00. www.youtube.com/watch?v=TYngD80CG6g&t=14s.

Kendi, Ibram X. 2020. "Who Gets to Be Afraid in America?" *The Atlantic*, May 12. https://www.theatlantic.com/ideas/archive/2020/05/ahmaud-arbery/611539/.

King, Lily. 2020. *Writers and Lovers: A Novel.* Waterville, ME: Thorndike.

Kittle, Penny, and Gay Ivey. 2019. "Engaged in Young Adult Literature: A Conversation Between Penny Kittle and Gay Ivey." *The ALAN Review* (Fall): 8–15.

Kleon, Austin. 2010. *Newspaper Blackout*. New York: Harper Perennial.

Koenka, Alison C., Lisa Linnenbrink-Garcia, Hannah Moshontz, Kayla M. Atkinson, Carmen E. Sanchez, and Harris Cooper. 2019. "A Meta-Analysis on the Impact of Grades and Comments on Academic Motivation and Achievement: A Case for Written Feedback." *Educational Psychology* November 7: 1–22. doi:10.1080/01443410.2019.1659939.

Lane, Barry. 2010. "A Walk in New Delhi with Damian Cooper." Feb. 2. 2:59. https://www.youtube.com/watch?v=dnMuDCSy0K0.

Learning Network. 2020. "The Winners of Our Personal Narrative Essay Contest." *The New York Times*, October 6. https://www.nytimes.com/2020/01/07/learning/personal-narrative-essay-winners.html.

Liu, David Shiyang. 2011. "Ira Glass on Storytelling." Vimeo video, June 6. https://vimeo.com/24715531.

Locke, Steve. 2015. "I Fit the Description . . ." *Art and Everything After* (blog), December 5. https://www.stevelocke.com/blog/i-fit-the-description.

Lukianoff, Greg, and Jonathan Haidt. 2018. *The Coddling of the American Mind: How Good Intentions and Bad Ideas Are Setting Up a Generation for Failure.* New York: Penguin.

Mandler, Anthony. 2013. "Story of My Life." Official music video, March 13. 4:07. https://www.youtube.com/watch?v=W-TE_Ys4iwM.

Martin, Rachel. 2020. "'Running for Your Life': A Community Poem for Ahmaud Arbery." NPR.org, May 27. https://www.npr.org/2020/05/27/862339935/running-for-your-life-a-community-poem-for-ahmaud-arbery.

Mauldin, Lauren. 2019. "The Colors of His Addiction." *Los Angeles Times*, February 24. https://enewspaper.latimes.com/infinity/article_share.aspx?guid=e4f771f3-cc21-4978-a778-2d03b68ff4be.

Mehta, Jal. 2020. "Make Schools More Human." *The New York Times*, December 23. https://www.nytimes.com/2020/12/23/opinion/covid-schools-vaccine.html.

Miller, Lulu. 2021. *Why Fish Don't Exist: A Story of Loss, Love, and the Hidden Order of Life.* New York: Simon and Schuster.

Moran, Seana, and Howard Gardner. 2018. "Hill, Skill, and Will: Executive Function from a Multiple Intelligences Perspective." In *Executive Function in Education: From Theory to Practice*, edited by Lynn Meltzer, 25–56. New York: Guilford.

Morrison, Toni. 1971. "What the Black Woman Thinks About Women's Lib." *The New York Times*, August 22. https://www.nytimes.com/1971/08/22/archives/what-the-black-woman-thinks-about-womens-lib-the-black-woman-and.html.

Muhammad, Gholdy. 2020. *Cultivating Genius: An Equity Framework for Culturally and Historically Responsive Literacy.* New York: Scholastic.

Murray, Donald M. 1996. *Learning by Teaching: Selected Articles on Writing and Teaching.* Portsmouth, NH: Heinemann.

New York Times. 2020. "Art in Isolation: An Ongoing Visual Diary in Our Uncertain Times." *The New York Times*, June 24. https://www.nytimes.com/interactive/2020/03/25/opinion/coronavirus-art.html.

New York Times Magazine. 2020. The Lives They Lived. *The New York Times Magazine*, December 23. https://www.nytimes.com/interactive/2020/12/23/magazine/people-who-died.html.

Newkirk, Thomas. 2012. *The Art of Slow Reading: Six Time-Honored Practices for Engagement.* Portsmouth, NH: Heinemann.

———. 2021. *Writing Unbound: How Fiction Transforms Student Writers.* Portsmouth, NH: Heinemann.

Obama, Barack. 2020. *A Promised Land.* New York: Crown.

O'Farrell, Maggie. 2021. *Hamnet.* London: Tinder.

O'Shaughnessy, Lynn. 2021. "Federal Government Publishes More Complete Graduation Rate Data." *College Insider* (blog). https://www.cappex.com/articles/blog/government-publishes-graduation-rate-data.

Owen, Wilfred. 1965. *The Collected Poems of Wilfred Owen.* Edited by C. Day Lewis with contributions by Edmund Blunden. New York: New Directions.

Pitts, Leonard Jr. 2010. "Sometimes, the Earth Is Cruel." *Dallas News*, January 14. http://www.dallasnews.com/opinion/commentary/2010/01/14/leonard-pitts-sometimes-the-earth-is-cruel/.

Prather, Liz. 2017. *Project-Based Writing: Teaching Writers to Manage Time and Clarify Purpose.* Portsmouth, NH: Heinemann.

Reilly, Rick. 2007. "Gamers to the End." *Sports Illustrated Vault*, February 5. https://vault.si.com/vault/2007/02/05/gamers-to-the-end.

Reynolds, Jason. 2020. "Journeys to Literacy: Multiple Paths to Common Outcomes." Keynote address. Literacy for All Thirty-first Annual PreK–8 Literacy and Reading Recovery Conference (virtual), October 26.

Richter, Felix. 2020. "The Steady Rise of Podcasts." Statista, May 26. https://www.statista.com/chart/10713/podcast-listeners-in-the-united-states/.

Rief, Linda. 2018. *The Quickwrite Handbook: 100 Mentor Texts to Jumpstart Your Students' Thinking and Writing.* Portsmouth, NH: Heinemann.

Romano, Tom. 2000. *Blending Genre, Altering Style: Writing Multigenre Papers.* Portsmouth, NH: Heinemann.

———. 2004. *Crafting Authentic Voice.* Portsmouth, NH: Heinemann.

Rosenblatt, Louise Michelle. (1940) 2005. *Making Meaning with Texts: Selected Essays.* Portsmouth, NH: Heinemann.

Rosenthal, Amy Krouse. 2008. *Encyclopedia of an Ordinary Life.* New York: Three Rivers.

Rudge, Lez, dir. 2020. "Star Stuff." Narration by Namakula Nasejje Musoke. YouTube video, 1:47. https://www.youtube.com/watch?v=H7Ad5ujaODM.

Schmoker, Mike. 2020. "Radical Reset: The Case for Minimalist Standards." *Educational Leadership* 77 (5): 44–50.

Shore, Billy. 2006. "The Flags of Our Sons." *The New York Times*, August 4. https://www.nytimes.com/2006/08/04/opinion/04shore.html.

Smart Social. 2020. "Teen Social Media Statistics 2021 (What Parents Need to Know)." Smart Social, April 16. https://smartsocial.com/social-media-statistics/.

Smith, Clint. 2014. "The Danger of Silence." TED talk presented at TED conference, New York City, July. TED video, 4:22. https://www.ted.com/talks/clint_smith_the_danger_of_silence.

Smith, Frank. 1988. *Joining the Literacy Club: Further Essays into Education*. Portsmouth, NH: Heinemann.

Sousa, David A. 2001. *How the Brain Learns*. Thousand Oaks, CA: Corwin.

Stafford, William. 2003. *The Answers Are Inside the Mountains: Meditations on the Writing Life*. Edited by Paul Merchant and Vincent Wixon. Ann Arbor: University of Michigan Press.

———. 2013. *Ask Me: 100 Essential Poems of William Stafford*, edited by Kim Stafford. Minneapolis: Graywolf Press.

Staley, Tim. 2021. "Unruining Poetry." In *Imaginative Teaching Through Creative Writing: A Guide for Secondary Classrooms*, edited by Amy Ash, Michael D. Clark, and Chris Drew, 123. London: Bloomsbury Academic.

Turkle, Sherry. 2016. *Reclaiming Conversation: The Power of Talk in a Digital Age*. New York: Penguin Books.

Tweedy, Jeff. 2020. "Here's How Jeff Tweedy Writes a Song." *Rolling Stone*, October 6. https://www.rollingstone.com/music/music-features/jeff-tweedy-songwriting-book-excerpt-1070889/.

Twenge, Jean M., Gabrielle N. Martin, and Brian H. Spitzberg. 2018. "Trends in U.S. Adolescents' Media Use, 1976–2016: The Rise of Digital Media, the Decline of TV, and the (Near) Demise of Print." *Psychology of Popular Media Culture* 8 (4): 329–45.

Warner, John. 2018. *Why They Can't Write: Killing the Five-Paragraph Essay and Other Necessities*. Baltimore: Johns Hopkins University Press.

Wiles, Deborah. 2017. *Revolution*. New York: Scholastic.

———. 2020. *Kent State*. New York: Scholastic.

Wilhelm, Jeffrey D., Michael W. Smith, and Sharon Fransen. 2014. *Reading Unbound: Why Kids Need to Read What They Want—and Why We Should Let Them*. New York: Scholastic.

Wilson, Maja. 2006. *Rethinking Rubrics in Writing Assessment*. Portsmouth, NH: Heinemann.

———. 2018. *Reimagining Writing Assessment: From Scales to Stories*. Portsmouth, NH: Heinemann.

———. 2021. Workshop description, Don Graves Write Now Conference, March 20, North Conway, NH.

Winston, Ben. 2013. "22." Official music video, November 8. 4:03. https://www.youtube.com/watch?v=AgFeZr5ptV8.

Woodfox, Albert. 2019. *Solitary: Unbroken by Four Decades in Solitary Confinement. My Story of Transformation and Hope*. New York: Grove.

Digital Composition

Book Clubs

ESSAY

POETRY